THE WAY  LOVES

21 Stories of God's
Healing Love to a Hurting World

BY
PRESTON RENTZ

TABLE OF CONTENTS

Chapter 1

THE DESERT'S HEART

While on vacation Robert Bogucki set out across one of the world's largest deserts despite warnings from the locals. He had a reason for his wandering, however. Questions about love and truth had been stirring for years, especially in regard to God's love and acceptance for him personally. And those questions needed answering once and for all.[1]

Determined to get those answers, Robert began his trek across the desert alone. Whether he would ever come home or come to some revelation about God's love for him remained to be seen. Robert and the rest of the world, however, would soon find out.

His choice of wilderness was the Great Sandy Desert of Australia. A vast landscape of sand, jagged rock formations and random pockets of vegetation, all of which covered about 300,000 kilometers (about 200,000 square miles). Very little of the vegetation was edible. Water was scarce, and few spots offered themselves as respites from the unmerciful sun.

In many respects, this environment stood in absolute contrast to the idea of love that Robert was in search of, including the gentleness and safety usually associated with it. The desert had its own appeal, however. Open spaces with plenty of room to roam must have felt like freedom. And few distractions, along with real privacy, must have given him time to think. Robert would soon discover the desert's dangerous allure, its rugged beauty along with its brutality. And even though he ventured headlong into an almost certain death trap, the questions of love remained at the forefront of his mind.

With only enough food and water for about a week, Robert slowly dragged his feet across the vast desert floor. He ended up walking about 250 miles in forty-six days by some accounts. As his provisions ran out within the first few days, he often had to dig for water and eat various vegetation springing up from the desert floor. When he was found, it was reported that he hadn't had water in twelve days. Though emaciated and weak, his health was remarkable considering all that he endured. The hospital that treated Robert said his good condition was a miracle. They were clearly surprised he had survived.

And when asked if he'd found enlightenment he replied, "Before I started out I really didn't know what I was looking for. I really felt alone, not desperate but just without hope at some point." Bogucki wanted to "make peace with God." He later indicated in an ABC radio interview, "I think . . . the feeling I have right now is a feeling of confidence that God'll take care of you."[2]

Robert's level of vulnerability and reliance on God was remarkable—and of great inspiration to me personally. His confidence had been renewed as he put body, mind, and spirit on the line to make peace with God. Robert Bogucki found God to be a help in a time of true need, and that His love is real.

The Question at the Heart of Each of Us

Somewhere deep inside I believe we are all asking the same question as Robert: Does God love me personally? Some may even be asking: Is God a God of love in the first place? And if He is, where's the evidence for such a love in the dark, corrupt, and violent world in which we live? And as I have often wondered: Is God's love for the religious only?

Each of us see, experience, and need love in different ways. Therefore, I will use a variety of stories, circumstances, occurrences, and world events to show the varied nature of our God and His love, and how He so skillfully weaves his love through just about any situation, event, or occurrence in our lives—and often in "nonreligious" ways. The truth is, God can speak through any means He chooses. And that is much of what *The Way He Loves* is about.

By the end of this book, I believe you'll more clearly see at least some of the surprising ways in which God shows His love and reveals Himself, and how this love continues to upstage the hatred and dysfunction that seems to plague our world.

Everyone's Journey

I believe that even the most hardened souls among us have a profound need to be loved and accepted. It is not obvious with everyone, of course; many have found clever ways to hide their human vulnerability and hunger for acceptance. But this need is innate in all of us, even if we do everything within our power to hide it.

Because of fear, broken trust early in life, and a million other reasons, some will hide their vulnerable side with an outer countenance of toughness, self-preservation, and an I-have-it-all-together persona. I've been there myself. When we're hurt or feel rejected, we want to run and hide, or just pretend we're okay. But beneath the rough exterior and our clever facade, each one of us is deeply vulnerable and in need of approval. The only real acceptance and love that will truly give us peace comes from our God.

As Robert Bogucki discovered, I find that no journey is more worthy of our embarking upon than this quest to know and experience God's consistent love—a love that matters more than any human love or romance we could ever experience. Few of us will brave a long and perilous excursion across the desert floor to discover full acceptance from our God. But we all enter the proverbial desert in our own way. For some of us, our desert is spending years alone and not letting anyone near us. For others, it's keeping God Himself at a distance, never really seeking Him or letting Him in. Others try and live a safe life, thinking that if they risk nothing, guard their hearts, and stay low, they'll avoid the pain of both love and loss. I know so many who live this way.

Yet others may bury themselves in pleasures of the flesh, attempting to anesthetize with alcohol, drugs, or some vain pursuit. Even noble pursuits can be an attempt to avoid the reality of our need for personal affirmation from our Creator. But the ache of both needing love and sealing oneself off from love continues. And so goes the dilemma, and its apparent contradiction.

Mere rumors of love keep many of us basking in the sunlight of hope, however fleeting that hope may feel. In my own long and painful journey to find a reliable and true love, I have found these rumors to be authentic and never to be abandoned. However, love and truth go hand in hand, and must be sought together so that we may know love's true nature.

Regardless of where you have been or what you've been through, my goal is to help keep your search for truth-based love alive, or to help you embark on this journey once again. Maybe even for the first time. Either way, welcome to the pursuit of real love. God's love.

However, I want to be clear: this is not a book about romance with another person. Most of us want this, and it can be a great blessing from God. But ironically, that particular journey itself can keep us from knowing and experiencing the Creator's love, which comes only from God Himself. No one human being can ever truly meet that innate need for real acceptance at the deepest levels of our being, and we are unwise to expect that from another person. The very best among us is limited in their ability to see, understand, and meet our needs at the deepest level of our souls. No, that is reserved for the One who *created* us. And as we seek God for this authentic love we're in a much better place to experience a healthy love with another person.

If you look for love in your Creator first, you'll find it. God is faithful to those who seek Him wholeheartedly. Too many have stopped looking, and that is tragic—but that is not you. I believe you're reading this book for a reason, and that you'll keep searching.

We are made for love, and instinctively we know this. We are drawn to its allure. But we are also plagued with the reality of its risk or cost. "What if I take a chance on love and it doesn't work out?" "What if the idea of perfect love is not real, but only the creation of talented writers of fiction and storytellers from long ago?" These questions, along with feelings of fear and doubt, make us leery of the pursuit and skeptical of love's reliability, even a godly love. The goal of this book is to show you God's faithful love, and just how ample the evidence of His love is.

We can step back and refuse to put our hearts on the line. And if we do, it's understandable because of past failures and pain. I've been there, too. Recoiling from love's possibilities, however, creates a much worse pain, for its very landscape is also desert-like, isolated, and laced with certain loneliness. This desert has no meaning because the possibility of love has been abandoned. Therefore, the suffering is even worse.

So, if we're going to take a risk—a leap of faith—the pursuit of a godly love is the only thing worth seeking and gambling on. As the heart becomes set upon love and we refuse to give up, the journey becomes more meaningful. God is good and will reward those who seek Him with a lasting love, a love that never falters or ends.

We must remember, "God is love" (1 John 4:8). In my long Christian walk, I have found this biblical declaration to be faithful and true. But God does require one thing, and that is that we seek His love from a place of faith, and with our whole hearts.

Robert Bogucki went on a quest to feel close to God, to feel God's love, and to achieve a sense of peace—and he was very happy with the answer. If you stay with me through this book, I believe you'll be happy with the answer too.

So together, let's bridge this gap between whatever is keeping you from knowing this great love, and making God and His love the very center of your life.

Reflection Questions

In what ways have you entered your own "desert" in order to discover and experience God's love, and be at peace with Him?

Does the idea of true love from God seem real to you? Where are you in your own journey in discovering that love?

What differences are you able to see between a love from God, and that of another human being?

Chapter 2

BEYOND THE CLAY

*H*e was the world's biggest movie star. His presence adorned the big screen with a boldness not familiar to moviegoers of his day. Restless mannerisms stirred curiosity. Facial expressions donned unusual determination. And his captivating gaze earned your full attention. The mere shifting of his large blue eyes alone qualified as an action scene. His presence on screen was nearly hypnotic.

The talented actor's career path was stellar from early on. Films such as *The Great Escape*, *The Magnificent Seven* and *Bullitt* helped establish him as a star of undeniable prominence. He made more money than most will ever see and reached a level of notoriety most will never experience. He was on top of the world, or at least at the top of his profession.

And yet his demeanor suggested something other than being on top. Rather, a heaviness of spirit did its best to shove him to the bottom. Apparent for all to see, there was more going on inside the mysterious persona of a Hollywood icon known as Steve McQueen.

Amid the celebrity, accolades, and access to just about anything, an emptiness persisted. A hunger raged like an out-of-control fire in the hills of Southern California. And memories of a troubled childhood haunted like a B-rated dark drama. Despite how far he had come in movieland, his troubled youth failed to remove itself entirely from his new designation as a Hollywood star.

McQueen was born in 1930 to a couple who fancied one another's company. They preferred sitting on perfectly good stools while leaning on the bar's edge. With bottle in hand his parents reminisced, perhaps about the fact that the stock market had just crashed the year before. And yet here they were with their new baby boy.

For many during those days, the local bar was more accessible than the human resources department of most employers. Jobs were scarce. Good paying jobs were scarcer yet. And a stiff drink was there to cast a soft glow on a harsh reality: the onslaught of the Great Depression of 1929.

Providing for a family in those days was a bleak prospect. As a result, perhaps, McQueen's father would soon abandon their mother along with young Steve. As the years went by, and because his mom was in and out of his life, McQueen did some of his growing up in a boy's home.

Feelings of unworthiness plagued McQueen from early on. Thoughts of anger from such a loveless past would secure themselves in the soul of a boy who never knew his father. In an audio interview McQueen once stated, "When a kid doesn't have any love when he's small, he begins to wonder if he's good enough. My mother didn't love me, and I didn't have a father. I thought, 'Well, I must not be very good.'"[3]

A sadness hung over his eyes, one which even the most gifted actor could not conceal. His serious countenance was so prevailing, in fact, that it helped shape a Hollywood archetype that incited great empathy from onlookers. Admiration even. And for many, relatability. Moviegoers probably sensed his pain, and many were drawn to his authentic nature, however downcast. Without Hollywood and moviegoers being aware, the concept of the mysterious but troubled hero was being molded right before our eyes. And there was a truth in this newfound hero, and in McQueen himself. But that truth would take time to surface.

The Transformation

In his book *Steve McQueen: The Salvation of an American Icon*,[4] Greg Laurie relates the amazing true story of McQueen, who started life out in the throes of poverty and dysfunction only to eventually find notoriety among Hollywood's elite. It is a tale worth telling—and perhaps a lesson worth learning. McQueen would soon discover the emptiness and folly of Tinseltown, and the unrelenting pressures of being a top star. A lot was gained, but a lot was lost as well.

The elusive promises of fame amidst the evaporating nature of monetary success continued to sneer at his unquenchable spirit. Many were after his celebrity for their own film project, but McQueen was after peace and solitude, and the two agendas collided head-on. The many film opportunities presented to McQueen eventually became a burden to the often moody and difficult star.

Like so many in the Hollywood game, McQueen found that success came with a price tag, and loss of privacy and freedom were the bulk of it. Some find this to be more loss than gain, and abandon this sometimes futile path altogether. McQueen was one of them. He would do nearly anything to get his anonymity back. His level of success, however, made that notion nearly impossible. But just as his story did not begin in Hollywood, it would not end there. And with no real personal connections, he soon found himself fleeing the film industry—and Los Angeles itself—entirely.

A Higher Calling

While working on films early in his career, McQueen discovered that some of his castmates were Christians. He did not like them much; they seemed peculiar and out of sorts with those around them. Though he was not kind to them, something caught his attention. There was a joy about them, and it left an impression that never went away.

As the light of worldly success grew increasingly dim, McQueen began asking questions—not only about Christianity in general, but about the Bible and this person named Jesus. And for the first time, a light began to grow brighter in a soul that had been dark for so long.

God would eventually bring a man into McQueen's life who would not only tell him about God the Father but would be a father-like figure in a way he never knew. Their relationship grew, and this brought great joy to McQueen. Soon after, McQueen began to visit a local church in a small town in California. While attending, questions about fatherly love and Christianity began to stir like never before.

This humble church was not attended by thousands, and the pastor was not a famous author or celebrity. But he answered McQueen's questions about Jesus and the God of love. A simple calling in a simple church was the setting for McQueen to give his life over to God's loving will. For him, a new life had begun.

Barbara Minty, his wife during the latter part of his life, would speak of the remarkable transition that took place in him over time. Minty noted that he was simply not the same person after he had given his life to the Lord Jesus; a peace and joy came into him that did not exist before.

As I watched the documentary *Steve McQueen: An American Icon*, also co-written by Laurie, a different McQueen clearly came to the surface. A renewal of the inner person occurred right before the viewer's eyes. And real joy enveloped his being. And in recorded interviews not long before his death, McQueen expressed his desire to tell the world what he had found in his newfound Savior.

McQueen's life was well documented in both photograph and film for millions to see. He was now on a different kind of stage, however, one few Christians see—not only as a famous actor but as one who would choose an authentic love and connection with the Creator over the sometimes phony associations of this world.

Steve McQueen's story is your story, and my story too. We may not have had parents exactly like his. You may or may not have spent time in a children's home. And you may or may not be a movie star. None of that matters. Whatever your story, God brought you into this world, allowed you to see its empty and futile ways, all that you may know His life-giving love. And to show you that godly love far outweighs anything this world can offer. If we are willing to accept that this is the reason for our lives, they will take on new meaning.

The Patience and Gentleness of God

I'm amazed by the fact that McQueen had access to the very best this world had to offer, and yet found God's love to be far more valuable. With all he had achieved, that's pretty amazing. As the famed actor Mel Gibson stated in an interview about McQueen, "the novelty of fame and wealth wares off pretty quick."[5] But as McQueen himself found out, God's love is lasting and never fades.

I'm also moved by the fact that God didn't seem in a hurry with McQueen, and wasn't forceful. He let him make his own choices, seek out his desires, and even prosper from them. And in the process, He allowed McQueen to see the futility of it all, and the emptiness that always follows. There was no manipulation. No need to rush. And no condemnation. Just a gentle nudge in the direction of truth, freedom, and the filling nature of God's love.

Things got messy throughout McQueen's life, and his behavior was reckless and unwise at times. God had committed, however, to bringing McQueen home, and never wavered. And in God's faithful love, McQueen was taken home in November of 1980.

The Sufficiency of God's Love

As I think about Steve McQueen's journey, I am reminded how complete God's love is. Nothing else could ever take its place. And knowing that His love is available to us regardless of what we have been exposed to or what our past may be is, well, remarkable. With God, it just does not matter. Wherever there's pain and emptiness, God fills it with His healing love. But we must turn toward that love if we are to know its comfort and favor.

My own upbringing was painful at times, for a variety of reasons. Maybe yours was too. Or maybe your source of pain came from somewhere else, or someone else. Whatever the source, even your own mistakes, God's love renders our hurtful past irrelevant. His love heals our wounds and binds our broken hearts—and even more so as we turn to Him.

Steve McQueen had achieved great worldly success prior to knowing God's love, a success that many marvel at and envy to this day. Our loving God, however, desires to take us beyond the success of the world and into a realm of peace and fulfillment that cannot be experienced any other way.

We are made in fact to go beyond the clay, beyond this mere physical existence of ours, and to experience His love in spirit and truth. When we do, we are truly transformed. We are truly filled.

Reflection Questions

What particular parts of this story could you relate to, or stirred your heart?

Did you receive the love and nurturing you needed in your own upbringing? Explain.

If not, what things of this world did you pursue in hopes of filling that personal void? What did you come to learn about those things that you once hoped would make up for the empty places in your life?

Chapter 3

TO GIVE YOU A DAY

*T*he morning sun glistens with hope. Its warmth stirs optimism. And its faithfulness proves that anything is possible for those who believe. Having grown up in the south, South Texas that is, I've come to treasure the sun regardless of its effect on the mercury, or my aging skin. As much as I value the sun, however, there are times when a gentle rain can soothe a weary soul. And the sound of raindrops colliding with the earth echoes the cadence of much needed calm.

The attraction of winter's soft glow continues to lure me, especially as autumn sets in. As the earth shies away from direct sunlight in the fall and winter months, the gentler light lands softly upon gilded leaves and browning landscapes. And as winter brings in the slumber in hibernation, cooler winds and leafless trees never fail to capture a reflective mood.

All the seasons speak in their own voice and deliver their own message—but only for those who take notice. Various thoughts and inspirations stir upon their arrival, as a sense of new horizons stake their claim near the perimeters of one's heart. And as age creeps in, I grow increasingly in tune with the proverbial sounds each season brings—pleasant sounds of hope laced with eternal promises of life forevermore, all confirmed by both the arrival and the depature of each season. Somehow I know it's the voice of God beckoning the seasons, a voice only the truest part of me can hear.

Whatever your ideal day or season may be, or however it may move or speak to you, it's no less than stunning what must occur behind the scenes so that they may exist in the first place. and that each and every part of our day performs as commanded. The mechanics behind the miracle of each day, in fact, are a marvel in themselves.

The Mechanics behind the Art

All three of our daughters are showing promise as artists; our oldest has a gift that was apparent from age four or five. With only pencil and paper in hand, each of them can make a blank page come to life with people and animals in a matter of minutes. As they hone their craft and learn from artists who have perfected *their* own craft, our daughters have learned an important truth: great art is not created by random or spontaneous strokes of pen or brush, but rather by skillfully learned and applied techniques. Great art is only good because the right techniques have been applied with skill.

In a way, this is also true with the art that has become any given day. And in this case, our loving Creator is the artist.

Our solar system operates as a gravitational system centered around the sun, which consists of the earth and seven other planets. These mostly desolate spheres' orbits are on a slightly oblong track around the sun. And they're all different, and in various ways. Mercury, Venus, and Mars are mostly made of rock and metal, and other minerals. Each vary in size and the types of metals they hold, and some of these metals don't exist on Earth. Jupiter, the largest planet, along with Saturn are mostly made of hydrogen and helium. Uranus and Neptune are mostly ice, but also include ammonia and methane.

The various sizes of these planets, their given substances, and their effect on gravity here on Earth all play a crucial role in sustaining life on the planet we call home, and with remarkable precision. Everything about these planets, including their detailed orbit system, are set into motion with intentional design. The entire solar system is fine-tuned to an incredible degree so that you and I not only have a sustainable environment in which to live a full life, but one that we may simply go about our day safely and joyfully. Yes, the sole purpose of this remarkably complex system serves one main purpose: to give you and I a beautiful day.

From sunup to sundown, and throughout a twenty-four-hour cycle, all things work together in our planetary system so that our air, light, and gravitational pulls make life not only possible here on Earth, but highly functional for the weather and seasons we enjoy.

Even our moon plays a role. It is placed perfectly in its orbit that it may break up what's called the mean motion resonance from the gas giant planets, which affects the angular speed in the orbit of these larger planets. Without our moon, the complex orbit system of these larger planets wouldn't quite work as needed. Everything has a purpose. Nothing is random. Everything is important.

In fact, the slightest infraction with the smallest player would throw things out of balance, and our finely adjusted solar system would change for the worse. The more we learn about our detailed solar system, the more we discover what a marvel its construct is, and how brilliant its design, and its designer: our God.

Earth is unique in the universe as far as we can see—and we can see deeper and farther into space than ever before. The deeper we look, in fact, the more we confirm this to be true. But we must understand that our earth is unique because our sun is a unique star. There is no other star known that would allow a planet to orbit it, and to have the complex level of life sustainability our earth has. The earth/sun relationship and their proximity to one another is unique to anything else we know of in space. There is no twin to either the earth or our sun, and astronomers have been looking now for at least sixty years.

The earth may be one of the smallest planets, but don't be fooled by its lack of mass grandeur. The entire solar system and the rest of the universe all play a role to not only make Earth livable, but also to protect it from powerful gamma-ray bursts, solar flares, and other objects and phenomena that may otherwise harm our planet, and us. The mostly invisible force fields around the earth's atmosphere protect the earth from such intruders and are only recently better understood by scientists.

It seems our loving Creator has gone to a lot of trouble to set a lot of independent objects into motion and juggle various elements so that we may have a sustainable home. In response, perhaps, we can celebrate His love, faithfulness, and generosity toward all His creation.

Walk outside, look around, and give God praise and thanks for all He's done, and for using his brilliance and skill that we may know His faithfulness, His love, and all He's willing to do in order to give you and me this amazing day.

What an amazing way He shows His love.

Reflection Questions

As you look at creation all around you, what begins to stir in your heart?

What do you feel creation tells us about God's heart, and how He feels about human beings?

As creation is a part of God's voice, what might His voice be saying to you personally?

Chapter 4

THE FATHER'S JOURNEY

*O*nce upon a time, there was a man and woman who married and had three children. They lived in a simple but spacious home in the country and were devoted to raising their children in love and truth. While they were still young, the father was compelled to know each of his children individually, and discover the unique gifts and passions they had received from their Creator. He decided that the best way to do this would be to take a special trip with each of them—one designed for that child alone.

One hot summer day, the father and his first child set out for their journey together. They walked upon the shores of vast oceans, explored beaches of powdery sand and roaring waves. They observed the movements of the tides, along with the seagulls that effortlessly glided over sparkling waters. Then they visited some of the great rivers that found journey's end at ocean's edge. They pondered how these rivers contributed to the ocean's vast water supply, and its delicate ecosystem. The complex system of rivers, lakes, oceans, and underground aquifers moved both father and child. They stood in awe of its silent deep and discussed the mysteries that must lie under her covers of blue.

After their first adventure, they went high into the mountains, rested in a small cabin, and considered all that they had seen. And, together, marveled at all that God had done. Then they searched their own hearts for the meaning of it all. After this, it was time to go home.

The father then took the second child on their journey. Together they took narrow trails across high mountain tops, braved rocky ravines, and negotiated dangerous pathways through the mountainous divide. The mountain peaks themselves were beyond majestic, as they stood face to face with other peaks strewn out over hundreds of miles, as if just below heaven itself. Upon reaching Earth's tallest peaks, they inhaled as much of the pristine mountain air as their lungs could hold. Afterward, they too rested at a cabin high on a nearby mountain. There the father sought to understand his child's deepest longings, truest desires, and hopes for the future. Then, it was time to return home.

Finally, it was time to take the third child on their journey of discovery. This time father and child set out to explore the wonders of the forest. There they found long trails meandering through sunless routes. They negotiated various vegetation including strange bushes, odd-looking plants, and an undergrowth as thick as a rug from Grandma's living room floor. While surrounded by the uncomfortable silence of mystery's lure, strange sounds often emitted from the forest as if they had something to say. These sounds came from places not seen with the eye but detected by one's fear. The subtle but ominous force that accompanied the sounds was always near, as they made their way through dense layers of long-stemmed plants with oversized leaves. But with machetes in hand and eyes ablaze, they forged on with an unrelenting determination and surprising courage. The forest's beauty and reigning magnificence remained, however. And as he had with his first two children, they eventually found rest at a cabin at journey's end. Here they sought to discover their truest hopes, their greatest curiosities in life, and all the potential the future held. Then, it was time to go home.

This tradition of traveling with each child went on for years—every summer, in fact. But there were rules. Each child, for instance, was not allowed to share any details of their trip with anyone else, including their own siblings. The memories and experiences were meant for them and their father alone. And they were okay with this agreement—but only for a time.

Eventually, each child began to wonder about the trips their siblings were taking with the father, and if the others had a better adventure than they did. They suspected they were somehow being cheated out of a greater experience. So they came to their father in unison and asked if they could each share the details of their trips with one another; they explained that they wanted to alleviate their fears and confirm that all was equal and fair, and that there was no cause for envy.

But the father refused. He explained that those trips and experiences were for that child alone, and not to be compared to another. He asked them to trust him. But they burned in their suspicion and stated they would never again go on any trips with their father unless he revealed the details of all the trips to each of them. His heart was saddened, but he did not relinquish. True to their stance, however, none of the children took another single trip with their father. And soon, they found themselves estranged from their father entirely.

Growing Up

Eventually all three children grew up and made lives of their own. But the lingering sadness from losing the tender relationship they once held with the father began to take its toll. As a result, the emptiness became unbearable. They began to wonder what the solution might be for such a persistent discontentment. Family, work, and life in general had somehow lost its meaning.

One day, while the three siblings were hanging out, they began reminiscing about the amazing trips each of them once took with their father, of which they began to miss dearly. They didn't recall many details, but understood that those days were long gone. And while they disagreed with their father concerning his rules and expectations of each of them, they honored him by having never shared the details of each of their trips.

Finally, the three children went to their father and mother and told them how much they loved and missed them, and that they wanted to be right with them again. They also explained that they were again curious about the trips they once took with the father. They explained that they were now grown and had a right to know the details concerning each of their siblings' adventures. Furthermore, the increasingly bold children suggested that they should all take their adventures together, as a family, so that they could once and for all confirm that their suspicions were not warranted. They argued that this would finally put all their suspicions to rest. Though the father was dismayed at their enduring lack of trust, he relished their return home. He also saw an opportunity here, so he agreed to do as they asked.

The very next summer, the father, mother and three children set out on the adventure of a lifetime. Finally, each one would soon discover what their siblings were up to all those years ago, for they continued to be convinced that each sibling had a better experience than the other.

The father first took all three near the ocean, then across small brooks and creeks, through many great rivers and to see beautiful ponds and lakes throughout the land. The two children who did not make this trip originally were bored and asked why they had to endure such a mundane experience. They were not drawn to the open waters nor the various mysteries that were contained within.

But the child who took the trip originally was overjoyed at returning to what had been experienced with the father long ago. The child recalled how much they loved the beauty of the water and the many ways it was used throughout the land. Now grown, however, the child realized how frightening the dark and deep waters were, and that the swift rapids of the rivers stirred anxiousness. This child asked why the father would expose them to such danger and fear. The father then replied that he had purposely taken them on a path they were both drawn to, but also afraid of, "so that I could face that fear with you, hold and comfort you and reassure you that I would always protect you and be with you." The child breathed a sigh of relief and hugged the father with such intensity as if they would never let go. They now felt closer than ever before.

Then they moved on to the next journey. On this excursion, the father took everyone over the mountaintops, across great ravines, and through ominous mountain passes. The two children who didn't make the trip originally found it too difficult, treacherous even—and worse, meaningless.

The child who had taken the trip originally, however, was once again enthralled with the beauty and majesty of the mountain ranges and recalled trips with the father fondly. But as they reminisced, a fear of the rocky heights, dangerous ravines, and scary places began to fill the child's heart. So, this child asked the father why they were taken to a place that scared them and placed their life in danger. The father explained that he knew this child loved the mountains and would be thrilled at their beauty and majesty. But he wanted the child to see the real dangers of high and treacherous places and wanted to comfort and remind the child that he would always be there, and protect the child in times of need. This child waxed grateful for the wisdom and thoughtfulness of the father. And the two grew closer than ever before.

Lastly, the father took all three deep into the forest. The two children who had not originally taken the trip found it too dark, spooky, and without any pleasure or purpose. They wondered why they should have to endure such a dreadful and gloomy trek through the woods.

But the child who originally came to this place was thrilled at their returning. The child found the forest with its darker hue and mysterious sounds to be alluring—but also a scary place laced with risk and danger. So, the child asked the father why he would take them into such a dark and dangerous place. The father explained that he knew this child was drawn to a darker and more mysterious environment, and that the child would need the light of truth spoken to help lead out of the deception of such dreary and strangely attractive places. Upon hearing this, the child was overwhelmed at the wisdom and love of the father and was grateful for their time together. And they too grew closer than ever before.

Wisdom from the Journey

All three children now understood that in this life on Earth, fear would always accompany what they loved and were drawn to, and that what they were drawn to would always have its dark and risky side. And each child now understood why the journeys were different and meant for each of them alone. They felt foolish for envying the others' journeys—and worse, for not trusting the father and his guiding wisdom. They could now see it was about the father's love for them all along.

Upon realizing this, they hung their heads in sadness and regret because they had lost trust for their father even though he'd had their best interests at heart. And they realized that the lack of trust had brought great emptiness in their lives. They mourned at all that had been lost.

Each child was inspired to thank their father for his faithfulness. They apologized for losing trust and imputing wrong motives all those years ago. Because the father's love was great for them, however, he instantly forgave them and once again welcomed them into his loving arms.

With great joy, the father then gathered all three and asked if they were ready to see the cabin in the mountains that each of them visited at the conclusion of their trips together. Each child assumed they all rested at different places, but upon arriving at the cabin in the mountains they soon discovered that they all had rested at the same cabin at journey's end. Something was different, however. The cabin looked, well, bigger. With great excitement, each child ran up to the newly enlarged and improved cabin, which was now an enormous house with many rooms. With excitement they could barely contain, they asked what had happened.

The father explained that while they were no longer making the journey with him through the years, he and their mother came to the cabin in the mountain each year to make a new place for them. In his love and faith, he believed they would someday return to him. Now that they had, his plan for them could be known.

He explained that each of them had their own homes, offices, and all their life's purpose within its vast walls and throughout its large courtyard.

The father's three children, and all their spouses and children gathered in the great mansion together. They were told there would be a great supper to celebrate their arrival. And at this supper they would celebrate the life, love, hope, and freedom the father had been preparing all these years.

All the children began to cry tears of joy as they gave thanks for the faithfulness and forgiveness of their loving father, and the new kingdom of which they were now a part. In their hearts, they praised and honored the One who had never left or forsaken them.

And they lived happily ever after on the mountaintop with their loved ones.

The Beginning.

Reflection Questions

What evidence can you see in your own life that God the Father is guiding your every step?

If you think of the "father" in this story as representing our Father in heaven, are you comfortable with the image of a loving God? Why or why not?

If there was a father present in your upbringing, did you have a good relationship with him? What effect, if any, does it have on how you see your heavenly Father?

What do you think of the correlation between what we're drawn to in this life and what scares us? Have your fears kept you from pursuing what you feel called to do with your life? If so, how?

Chapter 5

MR. ROGERS GOES TO WASHINGTON

The tone in Washington DC is sick with the flu. Accusations laced with demagoguery are often hurled with animus. There's a spirit of division so entrenched in the inner workings of democracy that the idea of mere gridlock seems old-fashioned, even nostalgic. The clashing of ideals is so contrary to one another that the phrase "One Nation under God" is beginning to sound like a lost dream. As rough and discouraging as things are, I'm reminded that we've been here before.

A Time of Turmoil

The decade of the 1960s was not unlike our own, especially in terms of division and the clashing of ideals. The challenges during this time seemed more sinister in nature, however, and less manufactured. The civil rights movement, for instance, was in full swing while still being debated, and resisted. The debacle of the Vietnam War would cast a dark shadow over the country for more than a decade—and many of its graphic horrors were being openly displayed on television for curious eyes of all ages. Vietnam was the first major conflict in which realistic videos of the war could easily be viewed within the sanctity of one's own living room. The bitter disagreements, along with persistent protesting over this contentious war, divided us in such a way not seen for a hundred years.

President Kennedy was assassinated early in the decade, and many believe to this day that our own government may have played a role. As a result, an increased lack of trust for government continues some sixty years after Kennedy's death. These were bleak times, to be certain. Divisive times.

The Judeo-Christian values that once held sway in our culture were being questioned and openly mocked like never before. This flagrant disregard for faith and moral constraint were demonstrated through the hippie movement and music festivals like Woodstock. The mantra of the day seemed to be, "if something feels good, just do it, right or wrong be damned." Whatever lines that once existed between acceptable behavior and indecency were now being cast away by some like dirty clothes no longer fit to wear. This wasn't everyone, of course, but it was a movement that took hold and continues to this day.

Rampant drug use was on the increase. America's current appetite for both legal and illegal substances can be traced back primarily to the 1960s. Blatant nudity both in film and magazines found their main footing during this time, and it's continued to soar ever since. Abortions were on the rise as well, and on the road to becoming constitutionally protected by the early 1970s. Tense times, to be sure. It was a considerably harsh time for everyone, especially the young ears and tender hearts of that day.

Young or old, however, this was new for America. And many were dismayed at the direction she seemed bent on taking, a direction of decadence of the likes never seen in the US.

I was born in 1961, so was not aware of many of the issues mentioned above. I do remember, however, a sadness that loomed during much of my childhood—a mood of melancholy that persisted at home and in my extended family members as well. Happy and cheerful times were few, it seemed. And when they sprang up, they were short-lived. Maybe it was my family's natural disposition. Looking back all these years later, however, I believe it had a lot to do with the times in which we were living. Many of the cultural norms that were in place up through the 1950s were quickly vanishing, and this left many in our country confused, angry, and depressed. My parents were among them.

One individual in particular who was deeply troubled by the sudden shift in cultural norms noticed its effects on children. His name was Fred Rogers. He knew that in previous decades there were built-in protections for children. During World War II, for instance, one had to go to the theater to see newsreels of the war. Now that television was in most homes and the news on during early evening hours, children could see images they could not understand that deeply troubled them. So Fred set out to do something about it.

A Tough Senator Meets a Gentle Lobbyist

The year was 1969. A senator from the state of Rhode Island named John Pastore was about to hear a pitch from yet another lobbyist looking for tens of millions of taxpayer dollars. And the tough senator was up for the fight as a stoic guard of America's wallet.

As the hearing ensued, the senator's face donned with an expression that suggested an annoyance at having to hear the brave lobbyist's request. Though blunt in tone and slightly defensive in spirit, he waited for the pitch to be delivered. It appeared that the answer "no" was already dancing on the tip of the senator's tongue, and anxious to escape its tooth-laden chamber. One didn't make it in those days by being passive or sensitive. Therefore, the Senator was ready for whatever came his way. Then, the gentle voice made his case.

Fred Rogers was a little-known public television personality at that time, but already had a TV show for children called *Mister Rogers' Neighborhood*. He needed funding, however, to continue broadcasting his program. To make his case, he described his interaction with some of the children from his show, the questions they were asking, and the pain some were expressing during this tumultuous time. He went on to express his concern for their mental and emotional health, and the gentle love and nurturing they were in desperate need of. In large part because of what they were seeing and hearing on TV, and in discussions of adults around them. As I watched a video of Mr. Rogers making his case, however, it was his approach that mostly caught my attention.

As Rogers laid out his need for the funds, his mellow delivery marched forth with something between a gentle whisper and friendly conversation, yet uncompromising in its intent. He was demanding only in his convictions, not in his arrangement of words or attitude. Capitol Hill was unaccustomed to such a gentle but firm spokesman, and it appeared this was not what the senator expected.

Rogers saw himself as an advocate for those young and impressionable minds, and was concerned for the effects so much violence would have on their well-being. The country was in the middle of a massive cultural shift which caught many off-guard. It bruised many a tender heart. These were brutal times for anyone to live through or witness, especially for children.

Rogers simply wanted to offer kids a respite from the angst of the day through his program *Mister Rogers' Neighborhood*, and designed it to be as antithetical to the world outside as possible. As in our day, however, public television relied on taxpayer funds, grants, and donations. And, also as it is today, you sometimes have to go before Congress to get those funds approved. The request at that time was for twenty million dollars.

Senator Pastore was known for being a "tough sell." Guarding the purse strings of the US Treasury was a job he took seriously. And lawmakers of that day were far less likely to approve funding, let alone for the ridiculous requests that sometimes win approval today. To make matters more challenging, this was still the age where kids were to be "seen and not heard." Rogers had his hurdles to overcome in a culture in which voices of advocacy for children were few—barely a whisper, in fact. Child psychology was still in its infancy.

Rogers, therefore, faced the possibility that being concerned for the little ones would come across as overly pampering. He believed in his cause, however, and did not waver. Undeterred, he made his case for the massive sum of money—and asserted that America's children were worth every dime.

And to Rogers' credit, he understood that it's not just what you say, but how you say it. Tone, along with one's approach, matters. He was careful not to preach or display moral superiority. He spoke from the heart and conveyed compassion for the children— and yet, demonstrated anything but passivity.

The result was stunning. Little by little, the facial expressions and heart of Senator Pastore began to soften. His eyes lightened up, and his subtle sarcasm faded. The inevitable "no" that surely rested on Pastore's lips also faded, and then ceased altogether. The tough senator finally gave in, but from a place of willing participation. As if his own inner child appeared to have surfaced, he gladly joined Rogers in his concern for the young and tender hearts Rogers was there to defend.

Two unlikely figures from two ends of the political spectrum became partners that day—allies for the cause of children—and together, secured the twenty million dollars for *Mister Rogers' Neighborhood*.

The Power of the Softly Spoken Word

As I write these words in 2020, how I wish there were a Mr. Rogers among us today. We sure could use him now. Especially in a time in which being bombastic and accusatory seems to be the default tone of our day. It sometimes appears we've lost all perspective as to what is considered good and acceptable public discourse.

I first started paying attention to politics during the presidential campaign between George McGovern and Richard Nixon in the early 1970s. Since that time, our public tone has dropped into the gutter, has flowed out onto the dirty streets and has finally rested in the deepest canals underground, that which we call the sewer.

As I think about Rogers' tone and approach, I'm reminded of the power of using the right words, having the right attitude, and of showing respect and kindness even to one's adversary. In great contrast to what we're used to today, Rogers' approach was gentle. Sincere. Conciliatory and disarming. And his respect for Mr. Pastore was always present.

Rogers, however, didn't kiss up to Pastore. For this is not a message about flattery or playing up to people; that approach creates its own problems. Rather, he simply expressed his concern for children and made his case plainly, without reservation. This was not a battle of personalities or ideals, as is often the case today.

Rather, it was simply about the need for the most vulnerable in our society.

Rogers' approach reminds me of some advice Jesus gave to His followers two thousand years ago: "be wise as serpents and harmless as doves" (Matthew 10:16, NKJV). I wonder how different our nation would be if more of our leaders valued this advice and applied its wisdom. Our obsession for constantly showing others where they're wrong and making them look as bad as possible to others has become an unhealthy pastime, an immoral form of entertainment. As a result, it's wrecking our country and tearing us apart.

I understand that people need to be called out at times, and that some very harmful policies and ideals need to be revealed as the destructive, faulty ideas that they are. We can't turn a blind eye. And we certainly can't compromise what we know to be reliable and true. But our approach of personal destruction so often used today is eroding our souls and missing the point of healthy debate altogether. It's painful to watch as we go down this road. And what a foolish path we've chosen.

To the contrary of what's become common, Rogers' delivery was shrewd but kind, his approach intentional but caring. His tone was bold, but patient and carefully paced. He held back nothing in making his case, but never failed to give Pastore his due respect. Instead of wielding the blunt instrument of forceful and arrogant speech, he made his case with humility. And with a careful shrewdness, he set the stage for Pastore in such a way that had he rebuffed Rogers and rejected his concern for the children, he would have looked like a monster.

In the process, Rogers kept his own innocence by never losing his cool, welling up in pride, or hurling insults at others who may not have agreed. He brought out the better side of Senator Pastore, honored him publicly, and showed a deference that is rare today. As a result, a childlike side of Pastore rose to the surface like a flower rising through a crack in a concrete sidewalk, only to discover the gentle and loving light above. In the end, Rogers won not just the funds, but a fellow advocate for children. By showing respect, he made Pastore a friend, not a foe.

The art of finding common ground has completely left our culture, I'm afraid. Though I must admit, that is getting harder to do in some circles, and with some of the issues we're facing today. That said, we need a Mr. Rogers to come forth today. We need a lot of them, in fact—not just in our neighborhoods but in our media. In our city governments, state houses, and federal government. We need to become a gentler people again and learn to see each other as fellow Americans, even when we see things differently—and to recognize that we need each other. When we do, good will win. When we don't, evil will prevail.

I'm personally moved by how Rogers remained respectful while not apologizing for his noble convictions. He honored free will and never tried to force his way, and yet never batted an eye to his cause or acquiesced to the forces against him.

Imagine if more leaders in our country emulated the example of Mr. Rogers. Imagine if our highest profile politicians, business leaders, and activists embraced a softer tone. And, imagine if anyone of us who has been given a voice were more respectful, tempered in demeanor, and able to win over even the most ardent adversaries. Imagine finally if we all took the responsibility, regardless of our station in life, to treat everyone with the respect that we ourselves desire. What a different nation the US would become.

With Mr. Rogers' example, I'm reminded of what's possible when one seeks to inhabit a right heart and spirit. But I shouldn't be surprised: Mr. Rogers was a follower of Jesus and reflected His nature beautifully. Though he is no longer with us, this is a man from whom we can all learn a little more of the way God wants us to be, and how to treat and love others.

Reflection Questions

What stands out to you most about Fred Rogers' approach to debate and communication? (There are videos of the exchange between Pastore and Rogers online, if you'd like to view them before answering.)

Why do you believe Mr. Rogers' approach was so disarming? So effective?

In what ways can you apply his example in your own way of communicating with others, including those with whom you may disagree?

Can you see Jesus in Mr. Rogers' approach? If so, in what ways?

Chapter 6

LIFTING THE FOG

A heavy fog draped the entire city. Darkness reigned at noon. Those on foot managed the dense moist air while en route to work. And those in cars struggled to make out silhouettes of pedestrians through dirty windshields and frantic wiper blades. This was no ordinary fog, however: pollutants of various kinds had mixed with the moist air to create a toxic smog.

Unfortunately, conditions were perfect for such a weather phenomenon as this: a mixture of smoke from commercial chimneys, residential fireplaces, and motor vehicle exhaust. And the results were catastrophic.

The fact that the wind failed to blow that day in London didn't help matters. And the fact that it was December didn't help either. Collars were pulled high upon the necks of shivering souls as they groped their way through cold and contaminated air. The fact that it was 1952 wasn't good news either, because any effective legislative steps toward a clean environment had yet to be taken.

The locals refer to these events as a "pea-souper," because it colored the air to a yellow-blackish hue. The color alone was cause for alarm, and this air-quality event was the worst ever seen in London. Various pollutants—including sulfur dioxide along with particles of soot from coal, which was the primary source for fire-places at the time—poisoned the air, and was now wreaking havoc on the human respiratory system.

Initially, it was estimated about four thousand people died from the event. Later estimates, however, put residual casualty numbers at about twelve thousand—all from an event that lasted only three days. The great smog event in London is probably the worst weather pollution event in history. In the world today, however, there's a proverbial fog that persists with much darker implications.

A Different Kind of Fog

Since the 1950s, both Europe and the United Sates have taken effective steps toward cleaner air and the restriction of emissions from all types of chimneys. What has not improved, however, is the spiritual fog that plagues so many in our world today. I can primarily speak for the good ol' USA, but this may be true of other countries as well. In fact, our proverbial fog seems so egregious that the very fundamentals of right and wrong are in question. And the basic rules of decency we once held dear, both among the religious and nonreligious, are now being tossed out on their heads.

As a result, there's an increasing confusion about what's acceptable behavior in our society and what isn't. A muddling of the difference between what is considered decent versus indecent. What is ethical versus criminal. What is justified exposure of one's dirty deeds and what is mere slander. And it appears we are losing a healthy understanding in general of what are appropriate expressions of dissent and what is merciless demoralizing of someone with whom one may disagree. A fog of confusion, to be sure. If you're watching the goings-on in our world today, you can think of your own examples of confusion raining down. Below are just a few that stand out.

Blurring the Lines

There are multiple points at which our society is currently grappling with confusion and fogginess of mind. There was a time, however, when people seemed to know what to do and how to handle things, at least in general. The world has never been perfect, and there's always been some level of confusion for sure, but I remember when there was more of a consensus on how to handle difficult and challenging issues that our country faced, both locally and nationally. We seem to be quickly losing this ability.

One example is our increasing inability to address criminal behavior in our communities. One lawmaker comes along and says we need to get tougher on crime and create tougher prison sentences, or at least to enforce the laws already on the books. Then someone else comes along and says we're locking up too many criminals and need to release thousands of offenders back onto the streets. And lately we're being told that the criminal is not the problem—the police are.

Another example is our struggle to effectively navigate the use of alcohol in our society. There used to be a differentiation between acceptable levels of alcohol consumption and all-out drunkenness, and appropriate places to purchase and drink alcohol. This line has all but disappeared. The largest seller of alcohol in my home state of Texas is not the local liquor store or the bar down the street—it's our most popular grocery store chain. The alcohol section in our store is at least three times the size of the milk-and-juice section combined. There's an ice cream shop in our area that will lace an adult's ice cream order with alcohol upon request. No, it's not an ice cream shop for adults only; it's open during the day for families and children. And some barber shops are now offering alcohol while getting a haircut. As a society, we're hard on those who drive while under the influence of alcohol, and yet more places are offering it than ever before. Our promotion of alcohol is increasing while our open concern for alcohol abuse seems to be quieting. And in most cases, driving a car is inevitably going to be involved in the purchase of alcohol, along with its consumption. In our confusion and lack of consistency, have we lost our moral authority against drinking and driving, or any form of alcohol abuse?

Then there's our increased emphasis on outward appearance, and its supposed connection to our identity. There are appropriate levels of this, of course. But as the focus shifts mainly to how one looks on the outside, the concern for the content of one's character appears to be diminished. Sadly, this trend is reaching the highest levels of leadership in our country.

Some are shaping their bodies to perfection at the gym and painting themselves as if they're a canvas on an easel, all the while giving little consideration to who they are inside. If there's a balance here, we seem to have lost it.

Most of us see violence in our society as unhealthy. Seeing the realities of war and bloodshed on television news is often enough to turn one's stomach and break one's heart. And yet, many don't mind it being in their kids' video games, their favorite television programs, or in popular films. Where would the film industry be without violence? We celebrate violence in our entertainment while deploring its reality, but of course expecting our children to know the difference. But do they? We are paying a price for our contradictory stance, and it's getting uglier by the day.

There's a combative nature in our society today. I watched a video recently of a school board meeting at which parents could voice their concerns to the school board over various issues. All of the parents shown in the video expressed themselves through anger, a spirit of hostility, and uncomfortable levels of blame and accusation. Emotions were soaring and not well controlled. I certainly share the concerns over what many of our schools are doing and trying to teach our kids, and can relate to a sense of outrage. But there was little respect and almost no sense of decorum in this public meeting. Not a single person was able to make their case calmly, coherently, and with due respect. It was painful to watch and made me wonder what's happening to the spirit and tone of our country.

The trend I'm most concerned about, however, is existentialism, which may in part explain the tone of our day. This philosophy suggests that one can go through life concerning themselves only with their own sense of free will, and without acknowledgment of a Creator or whether it's considered to be right or wrong—and doing it irrespective to its effect on others. Service to self is top priority in this line of thinking, and is based on self-designated terms. I believe this cancer among us explains much of the lack of unity in our country today and is at the core of many of our problems.

There are so many others we could explore here. But it's important to note that the Word of God instructs us on these issues and many more. The purpose of this chapter is not to answer each one specifically; one can do that by simply reading the Bible and discovering its wisdom. Rather, it is to make the point that God gave us His Word so that we would not go through this life confused and wondering how to handle this or that issue.

From the beginning, God has been aware of our propensity to get into a foggy mindset over the challenges of life. After all, there are thousands of competing messages and philosophies coming at us from multiple angles every day. And in the US, this has never been truer. The Creator offers a solution, however, and reminds us there is no reason for groping around in a dense and polluted fog. All we must do is stop, take a deep breath, and let the fresh air of God's liberating truth fill our lungs, refresh our minds, and calm our anxious hearts.

Our Need for Clarity

There's nothing more miserable than going through life without clarity. Having a clear picture of what is true, reliable, and unchanging is liberating beyond words. When I think about the most painful time in my past, especially my upbringing, I can define it as lacking any real clear vision about life and what it should look like. And I believe that to be the case for many people today. We have an innate desire to see things as they are, in a clear light, and with hope for the future. So many people don't live with this simple recipe for a life filled with clarity.

Our country is in desperate need for leaders with clarity as well, and with wisdom that can be applied to all situations. Especially in our city leaders, mayors, governors, lawmakers, all the way up to the president, as well as in our schools. Wherever there are leaders who represent a sector of the public, we need them to lead with reliable ethics based in truth and respect for others, rather than with their own personal preferences, political biases, or the cultural trends of the day. Much of what we see today are not expressions of wisdom and maturity, but emotional rants based in fear and bias—often existentialism at work.

Clearing Up the Fog

By the age of 19, I was on my own and stumbling through life with no real direction—not only in relation to career choice but in what

I believed about life, truth, and even love. Those things were not defined for me during my upbringing. But that all changed when I came across the Bible. When I began to read the words inside and the stories of God's people and their given struggles, I knew I had come across real wisdom for life. As a result, an authentic knowledge and understanding of life, and the way it actually works, began to emerge. Confusion began to wane, for the first time in my life. And as I read about Jesus in the Gospels, the Savior of the world, I knew that I had come across the words of life. The God of life.

The words I read were compelling, laced with clarity, beaming with hope, and well beyond what I could have previously imagined. A reliable vision for real living was finally set before me. And its blazing words took hold of my heart.

As a student of the Bible now since 1981, I can attest to its consistent and reliable nature. For many years, I read the Bible as a skeptic, constantly looking for flaws and contradictions. Because of what I experienced in my youth, I didn't trust anyone or anything, including the Bible. But I was drawn to its pages of mystery and antiquity—mostly, however, its promises, especially the words of freedom, redemption, and love. And as hard as I looked, I was unable to find any falsehood or contradiction. To the contrary, I found the words of the Bible to be consistent, faithful, and true. And these amazing words have not only set me free with remarkable clarity, but have guided me through every tear and heartache throughout my adult life. The Bible is simply the most reliable source of truth for a free and vibrant life—and for a free and healthy society as well.

I trust the Bible because it's unpolluted by mere human opinion; it is unbiased and nonpolitical. Some criticize it because it was written so long ago, and therefore consider it out of touch with our own language and culture. Ironically, that's where its value lies. The Bible is not subject to the whims of the human thinking of our day or the ebbs and flows of cultural movements over time. It simply speaks of a truth that has always been true, and always will be true. People are people, no matter where they are from or in what period of history they lived. The same basic issues that people had thousands of years ago are the same issues of our today. Because of this, the Bible addresses human relationships as accurately as anything I've read from our own time, and more insightfully.

The Bible is simply the truest work on human nature and all its pitfalls. This has not only helped me to see myself in the light of truth, but to see others more realistically as well. As a result, it has helped me to avoid self-deception as well as the ill intentions of others.

Learning the truth of God's Word is freeing, because it reveals the delusions of life that so easily plague us and brilliantly keeps us from those trappings of falsehood that can so easily entangle us. Forty years after my initial reading of Scripture, I continue to be stunned by its level of precision and insight into all matters of life.

The Bible also puts the "here and now" into perspective. The past, present, and future are all addressed with remarkable lucidity and certainty, and always mixed with high levels of hope. I know so many people who either obsess over the past, can't see the beauty in the present, or are anxious for the future, and fail to enjoy this life as a result. The wisdom of God's Word, however, causes us to rest in the rhythm of time passing while basking in the glory of the present day.

While so many voices today speak of impending doom and gloom, God's Word offers authentic hope with a bright vision for our future, regardless of what's going on around us. One thing is for sure: if you explore its pages and spend time there, you'll discover the true liberation of seeing things as they really are. Reality is not our problem; a delusional perspective on reality is.

I've noticed that there's a certain ring to a body of literature that is true and factual. Likewise, fiction has a certain ring to it as well. And the Bible truly has the ring of truth to it. Yes, the Bible has a spirit about it that draws one in and rewards one for dropping by for a visit. So, embrace her and she'll become a faithful friend.

In its pages of mercy, love, and truth, the Bible invites the reader to test out what it claims so that one can confirm its reliability. Though God's Word propels us primarily to believe and trust in God, it mercifully also encourages us to put those words of life to work so that our faith may be confirmed. And in my time of doing just that, I have found it to be completely reliable, without flaw.

Perhaps not everyone will take the time to explore the words of life, freedom, and truth presented in the Bible, but I've noticed this simple truth: those who trust its unique compilation of stories, teachings, and wisdom are blessed in unusual ways. I believe you are one of those people, and that you are a seeker of truth through the words of life. You will be rewarded richly for doing so. You'll also find an authentic and purposeful life that will develop within and all around you, especially if you do what the Word of God compels its readers to do. What a generous gift our God has given us through His Word.

> All Scripture is God-breathed and is useful for teaching, rebuking, correcting and training in righteousness, so that the servant of God may be thoroughly equipped for every good work. (2 Timothy 3:16–17)

Just believing is not enough. And just claiming you're saved by grace alone isn't enough either. Both are important and true. But now that you have the foundations of faith and grace in place, you must use their power to actually seek the Word of God, learn to abide by its wisdom, and live by its words so that you may know life to the full. If you don't, the lies of this world have a way of creeping in.

If we as individuals and as a country begin to live by God's Word, we'll see healing and unity once again. There is not a single problem we're facing today that the Bible does not address or have an answer for, either directly or indirectly. And those answers are worth digging for.

Things may be foggy in your life right now, and in the world around you. Instead of trying to make sense of it on your own, delve into the pages of the Bible and let God's Word put things into perspective. It's hard to imagine this, but both the good and evil in our world serve a purpose, as both are guided by the wise hand of God.

God worked through many different authors over roughly 1,600 years to create the Bible, so that you may have the words of life. What a great act of love on the Father's part.

The greatest words of truth, life, and clarity await you. Get busy and learn them.

Reflection Questions

How much has the Bible been a part of your life so far?

What stories or scriptures from the Bible have stood out to you?

When have you found comfort or guidance in God's Word?

What would you consider to be healthy goals for reading the Bible and making it a part of your daily walk with Christ Jesus?

Chapter 7

WHEN GOD SPEAKS IN UNCONVENTIONAL WAYS

The movie was going to be just another romantic comedy, a re-spin of one of Hollywood's many movie templates. Another cookie-cutter story adorned with new faces and fresh dialogue, but still an old idea. The main plot, however, was not just a romance between two people. This film had another main character—a character, in fact, who rarely joins the cast. Who might this other person be? Well, "God."

The story line was about a guy trying to make a five-year relationship with his girlfriend work. However, a narcissistic nature, along with unbridled ambition for success, kept getting in the way. Lasting love and achievement may have been his dream, but a stubborn failure on both accounts was his reality.

The story eventually develops this character, played by Jim Carrey, into a person who gets frustrated with how "God" is handling things in his life, and the world over. He expresses his disapproval through dramatic displays of mockery and over-the-top arrogance, all in classic Jim Carrey style. What Bruce (Carrey) didn't expect however was that "God" had decided to call his bluff. "God" does this by giving Bruce the role of being "Him" for a while. And Bruce quickly finds out it's not as easy as he thought. You may already realize that the film we're discussing is *Bruce Almighty*.

Once I knew the essence of the story, it had my attention. This may not be the usual "sleep with whomever you choose with no moral consequences" type of romantic comedy after all, or the mere emotion-driven kind of love story that's often presented in films. So I sat back and anticipated a clever comedy with an unusual twist. And I was not disappointed.

The script was well written and the roles well-acted by several other talented actors, including Morgan Freeman and Jennifer Aniston. Because it had the "Creator" as one of its characters, I had to remind myself that it was a Hollywood production, not a film written and produced by a Christian seminary graduate; therefore, it wouldn't be fair to judge it by strict biblical standards or the finer points of Christian doctrine. Like most, I just wanted to enjoy a good movie. That said, I was not prepared for the impact this movie would have on me, especially regarding matters of God's grace and its effect on the whole world.

Before I saw the film, I knew of grace mostly in an academic way. After watching the film, however, my heart was aglow with the incredible generosity of God's rich forgiveness for anyone who wanted it. I was now seeing God's grace everywhere, and in a grander way than before.

What surprised me the most was how much the movie's point lingered—for days, in fact. This was no fluke. My heart expanded a little after seeing this film.

Bruce Almighty helped me to see the world around us in a new light—not just the metaphorical world consisting of people, languages, and culture, but our literal world and society. I could better see God's hand in the design of our cities, our crucial infrastructure, along with how commerce works to provide our needs. Without the creation of our minds by God, we could never design or build such structures. So, for the first time, my lens of the world had been altered to see that nothing of order or symmetry occurs without the graceful hand of God. I finally understood that all of it comes from the Creator, as a great gesture of love for humanity.

As individual Christians, it's easy to see our walk of faith from our own vantage point and how it affects us personally, or to believe that God's love and forgiveness is just for a select few. The film, however, took the viewer out of that micro or inward vantage point to show the opposite: the plight of the whole world from what might be God's perspective, and the billions affected daily.[1]

Services are provided, products are made available, and people's needs are met, all emanating from the merciful and generous hand of God. I'm not suggesting that our world is without flaw or not in need of improvement on many levels. It's an imperfect system, to be sure. I am acknowledging, however, that without God's sustaining hand, nothing would work as intended and things would be much worse.

More fundamentally perhaps, no human can laugh, breathe, love, or live except by the grace of God. He's our Creator, after all.

---

[1] I'm not advocating the theory of universalism here. I'm merely expressing the heart of God, as stated in Scripture, that Jesus died "for the sins of the whole world" (1 John 2:2) and that God himself "wants all people to be saved and to come to a knowledge of the truth" (1 Timothy 2:4). Scripture is clear, however, that the grace and forgiveness of God is enjoyed by those who repent of their sins and profess their faith in Christ Jesus, and suggests that not everyone will take advantage of God's offer of grace.

Life simply happens because of God's ongoing flow of love for the world, regardless of whether its acknowledged or perceived.

Keep in mind, this movie was a comedy. They didn't communicate all this with great depth or theological profundity. However, they didn't have to. The general message was clear. The goodness of God rains down to lighten our burdens and delight our souls, and is available to anyone who wants it. And in one way or another, we're all the benefactors of that goodness. Not everyone will accept this as true, or even want it to be. When it rains, many block it with umbrellas or run for cover. Others, however, just stand in it and let it soak them.

For at least a week, I was in a perpetual state of awe as I now saw God's hand in things I wasn't previously able to see. A hard heart can block wonderful truths, even when they're right before our eyes. I had a real "head to heart" experience after watching this movie. And I knew God had broadened my view of Him, and his goodness, in the process.

I've heard many great sermons, have read some amazing books, have pondered some deep and profound Christian theology and commentary, and still do. The wisdom of God is a deep well, and one with eternal implications. But this movie managed to show me a whole new level of God's desire to save the world through His profound love.

God Speaks through Anyone or Anything He Chooses

While God speaks primarily through His Word and through those in whom His Spirit dwells, He's not limited to these channels. God will never compromise who He is or His established Word. But we're all different, and have various desires, hopes, and dreams. He knows how to speak specifically to each of His children, and He'll use all of creation to do so.

Literature

Books or stories are another great way in which our loving God speaks to us, and with surprising levels of specificity.

One such book for me was *Journey of Desire* by John Eldredge. God used this book to help me link the Christian call with the deepest desires of our heart. I was previously very confused about this subject because of some previous teachings. There's a misunderstanding about the Christian faith that says that all desires, no matter what they are, must be abandoned for Christ, and that we're to live a bland, joyless, and passionless life in sacrifice for Christ. Of course, Scripture doesn't teach that. In fact, it teaches the very opposite. That way of thinking comes from a dangerous religious spirit, not from the Spirit of God, or His holy Word.

Part of walking with God is discovering the true desires He has put in us. This makes the Christian walk much more fulfilling than anything this world has to offer. Eldredge's book was certainly a catalyst for me to see this truth and to learn to trust what God's Word actually says about the Christian walk.

Les Misérables, the famous story written by Victor Hugo and first published in 1862, is one of the most enduring stories of all time. I feel as if I have a better understanding of the need for both grace and right living from this story. This classic book contains a rare combination of faith-based elements worth discussing, including legalism, grace, mercy, redemption, sacrifice, and many other Christian related themes. It's as if Hugo wanted to pit all these themes against one another so that we could see them in their true light, and see them outside of the paradigm of a religious setting. And by doing so he brilliantly reveals the trappings of legalism, the process of redemption, and the liberating quality of forgiveness from a loving God—something often unachievable in a sermon or even a series of sermons. This remarkable literary achievement is unsurpassed in both book and film regarding this subject matter, and is here to enlighten some 160 years after its initial publishing.

Another impactful book for me outside of Scripture is *The Jesus I Never Knew* by Philip Yancey. I read this at a particular low time in my life and learned to fall in love with the person of Jesus. Yancey doesn't preach, and uses no religious clichés. In a style likened to a journalist's, Yancey takes the reader out of the mere American version of Jesus and allows you to see Him internationally, historically, and as a real person who once walked the earth. God used this book to raise my faith above religious ideals and helped me to see our Savior Himself more realistically, and as our one and only deliverer.

Music

Music, of course, is another form of art that reaches a portion of our hearts that religious activity or classic preaching simply can't. Some classic hymns have moved me over the years, along with many modern praise songs. What's been surprising to me, however, is that some of the most moving and inspirational songs I've heard about God and His love weren't from Christian artists necessarily, and weren't even hymns—rather, from secular artists who happen to be believers in Jesus and have written and performed great songs of faith.

A good example of this is Hillary Scott's song "Thy Will." This song moves me every time I hear it. Hillary is the lead singer for the country music group Lady A. And yet, this song won a Grammy for Best Contemporary Christian Music Performance/ Song in 2017. It is an amazing song about trusting God's will even when life isn't going the way we want or thought it would. There is something special about this song, and it has clearly moved many people. It's as if it had a special anointing on it, but with no formal "Christian" label attached.

I continue to be moved by Christian songs from multiple sources, and it's been great to see the Christian music industry swell over the past forty years. But I continue to be inspired by the fact that God can stir our hearts and speak to us through whatever format He chooses.

Creation

I lived in East Texas for a brief period while attending college there. A long relationship had just ended, and several close friends had moved away. I was trying to sort out what my next step in life would be. Everything seemed to be uncertain, in turmoil. There were only inner rumblings as to what God had in store next, but no real clarity.

I went hiking one day around a pristine but small lake called Lake Hawkins. Parts of it were lined with rows of large pine trees. For some reason, the trees had caught my eye. I was captured by their majestic beauty and natural symmetry as they stood proudly on the lake's shore. It was a windy day. The tops of these tall pine trees swayed back and forth with every gust. No matter how hard the wind blew, however, the trunks of the trees stayed constant and remained unmoved. In that moment God used that imagery to plant a beautiful truth in my spirit: "The winds of life will blow, people come and go, circumstances change, and we will feel the effects of those changes. But God Himself is unmovable, and His love and commitment to you will never be swayed." After hearing that in my spirit, I was instantly at peace.

For the rest of the week, all I could think about was the faithful and loving nature of God: unchanging, consistent, and reliable. And I carried that truth with me as I went to the next part of my journey. This is the way our God loves.

These many years later I can still see those pine trees swaying in the wind, again reminding me that our lives at times will feel chaotic and uncertain, but that the God we put our trust in is never moved and that which matters most will not change, especially His love for His people. Though all this occurred in a matter of seconds, its memory lingers some twenty-five years later. More importantly, this truth continues to be reinforced in my life.

Some like to quote the old saying that says "the only constant is change." But I've learned that the one thing that matters most never changes, and that is God's faithful love. His love will never falter. Never fail. That is who God is. Let the world change, but God's love never will.

People aren't always faithful. Opportunities rise and fall. Doors open and close. Life sometimes has surprises. But God is as steady as a forest of age-old trees that refuses to be uprooted. And His steady nature sometimes shows itself best against a world of uncertainty.

Friends

Before I met my wife, I had a conversation with a friend about the age bracket I thought my future wife should be in. Uncharacteristic of my friend, he just stopped what he was doing, looked me in the eyes and boldly stated, "Who are you to decide which age bracket she should be in? That's God's job. Leave that up to God." I was stunned because of my friend's rare boldness. He never spoke to me like that.

About two weeks later I met the woman who would become my wife. She was outside the narrow age bracket I would have previously considered ideal. But my paradigm about age had been altered; otherwise, I would not have given this woman a second thought. And perhaps, she wouldn't have considered me. God knows how to prepare us for what's coming. If we're wise, we'll listen.

Shortly after my conversion to Christianity and still in my early twenties, a friend confronted me about cleaning up my language. There were a few words that sprang from my mouth that he didn't think were appropriate for a believer. (Okay, I'll just spill it; I cussed like a sailor.) And he was right. His bold confrontation got my attention and set me on a new path for choosing better words for expressing myself.

Another friend once told me the story of a very dark and confusing time in his life. At his core, he wondered if God really loved and accepted him. He went on a long walk through his neighborhood one day and was praying about this issue. Suddenly a car of young people drove by, honked their horn, and yelled out the window, "God loves you!" My friend stopped suddenly, welled up in tears, and realized that God had just told him what he really needed to hear through a car full of total strangers. The timing could not have been more perfect.

All the world, its people, and every aspect of creation is at God's disposal. And if we're open to it, He'll speak to us in surprising ways. Any way He chooses, in fact. I love the way God loves.

Failure

The only way in which I'm comfortable thinking back about my various failures in life is through considering all I've learned from them. I have narrowed down the need for occasional failures to this one crucial point: God wants to show us who we really are in Him and reveal the authentic self that is easily buried within us. To do so, He must expose the phony selves many of us try to live by and succeed from.

If God allowed us to be successful in something that wasn't God's best for us, or wasn't tied accurately to our identity, it wouldn't be a real success. It would only steer us further off the path God has for us. Remember, God is a God of truth. He's not into artificial anything. If you're going to walk and abound with Him, it will always be related to who God has made you to be, and no other version of who you are.

This may be one of the reasons why so many people have great success early in life but feel a disconnect later in life regardless of that success. I wonder if the well-known midlife crisis is linked to this issue.

The process and payoff of real success is so much more than monetary gain, prominence in the marketplace, or mere recognition for some achievement. These can be good, of course. But our success in life is meant to reveal so much more, something of much greater value in fact, and that is who we are as God's children and what our true roles in this life are supposed to be. Failure is an important part of that end goal, because it has a way of revealing the posing or pretending part of our nature.

When I think of businesses that failed, relationships that didn't work, or interests in life that didn't last, I'm immensely grateful for God's guiding hand that led me out of them. I wouldn't trade those experiences for anything. They were painful and confusing, but absolute gold in all they revealed.

When I look at new opportunities today, I always check my gut first and make sure they coincide with my personal values, who I am as a son of God, and all that I know about who God is still shaping me to be. If it doesn't pass that test, if it doesn't align with the path He has me on, then it's not a good idea. Learning to listen to how God speaks has improved my life tremendously, and has helped me to better recognize opportunities that are the right fit for me and my family. I'm grateful for this kind of love and guidance.

Successes

I equally appreciate what our loving God reveals through successes along the way. And one of those important truths is this: true and fulfilling success will always occur when we stay true to who we are, and do not allow distractions, greed, or other misplaced motives to get us off track.

This is how great and loving our God is. His heart desires that we not only pursue what we're drawn to in a healthy way, but to the things that are most aligned with who we really are internally, along with our God-given talents and desires. And when we do, our success will be meaningful, on top of any monetary gains or benefits otherwise.

Every time I finish writing a book, I feel a remarkable sense of accomplishment—even before a single book is sold or a single person is affected by its content. And in that first stage of success, there's an important truth that's reinforced: that hard work, good research, patience, and a lot of editing pays off in the end.

This also applies to being a better husband, father, and many other things in life. As I make good decisions and stay with what I know is right, truth gets reinforced and success begets success. These positive achievements have taught me that completing something is crucial, no matter how hard it is or how long it takes, especially if it coincides with our own personal path. This must occur if we're to endure and achieve something worthwhile. Only success can teach us that, and provide the kind of encouragement the Father desires to give.

God's idea of success is rewarding both externally and internally, both financially and spiritually. The success of the world, or a success that is a compromise to who we are in God, is only rewarding externally. But, in the end, it brings disappointment and emptiness—and in some cases, even personal corruption. I've watched too many friends go down this road. Success by the world's standards is never worth it because the cost is always more than any perceived gain. Compromise has a way of catching up to us.

I continue to check my gut and make sure the various ventures I'm into today are a good fit, and that they are closely tied to who I am at my core. I've finally learned that if an opportunity doesn't fit this criteria, I leave it behind.

Many say that God teaches us more in our failures than our successes. That sounds clever, but this simply isn't true. Lessons are to be learned and great truths revealed in both failure and success. And this life will always include both for this reason. The greater lesson, however, will always be gained by doing what's right, because it is tied to obedience. This requires trust and faithfulness—both of which are their own reward.

We need successes along the way because they remind us what's reliable and true—and that compromise is never worth it. Never. And our loving God speaks volumes through these deeply rewarding experiences in life.

Don't let regrets get you down. Our regrets in life may be the best reminder that we needed to redirect and walk a truer path. God is certainly speaking through them. However, doing what's right will always reap a better harvest.

Learning to Listen to the Voice Inside

Everything we've been talking about here is learning to listen to that inner voice, and to know that its promptings can come at any time and through many different sources, if not our very own consciences. Somewhere along the way, I started noticing that when

I ignored God's subtle but present voice, I always regretted it. I've come to respect its remarkable accuracy and reliability.

If any kind of impulse or inner voice ever suggests we do something contrary to Scripture or what we know to be true about God, it should be ignored and rejected. The Word of God warns us to test all spirits or compulsions to make sure they are indeed from God.

If we're walking in truth with God, however, that inner voice will be the Holy Spirit guiding us. What a remarkable way God speaks to us, guides us, and shows His love for those who trust in Him.

Reflection Questions

How can you relate to some of the ways God has spoken to the author, as outlined in this chapter?

Do you feel God is speaking to you through music, sermons, the Bible, Christian books, movies, etc.? Explain.

What are some of the ways in which God has spoken to your spirit recently, or in the past?

Can you see that if God does speak to us, it will always align and agree with His holy Word, and will always involve His love for you, and love for others? What examples of this can you think of in your own life?

Chapter 8

EXPRESSIONS IN THE COSMOS

One of my childhood homes sat on forty-three acres in a remote part of the Texas Hill Country. Climbing on the roof of that house to view the stars with my father was one of my favorite things to do. The darkness around our house on those clear nights was complete. It seemed like we were surrounded by massive black walls. Not a single streetlight or porch light could be seen. The only light was the moon and stars.

While lying on the rough asphalt shingles, Dad would try to explain how far away the stars were. I tried to comprehend the distance, but it only hurt my brain. He'd also talk about our solar system and its planets. The most memorable part of those nights decades ago was his telling of the God who created it all. He presented God in a caring and loving light, and that stuck with me. I could have laid on those uncomfortable shingles for hours.

My faith in God began on that roof. But not all stargazers are believers—including one of the most famous stargazers of our time.

Stephen Hawking

Hawking, a renowned theoretical physicist and cosmologist, was known for his work on gravitational singularity theorems, black holes, and quantum mechanics, among other cosmological interests. But he was best known perhaps for his book *A Brief History of Time*. First published in 1988, it stayed on the *New York Times* bestseller list for 237 weeks, and eventually sold more than 9 million copies. It was popular in part because it put many of the new discoveries concerning space and time in common terms. Most could now read and enjoy the latest understanding of how our known universe theoretically came to be.

Hawking believed that God didn't exist, at least not in the personal sense the way Christians and Jews do. Though he occasionally referred to science and creation itself as a type of god, he was a self-proclaimed atheist.

When one reads Hawking's own statements about the universe and the challenge of intelligent design, however, one may sense that Hawking struggled to explain the degree of specificity to which the universe was created while maintaining that it somehow came into existence randomly on its own.

Mounting Evidence

Whether one believes in a Creator or not, evidence is mounting in favor of the creationist. The deeper we look into space, the more we comprehend its complex history, design, and functionality—and the more it looks like the universe had to be designed with intent from a source outside it, and with nearly unimaginable degrees of precision.

Some highly intelligent atheists are coming to the same conclusion, to which they have no choice if they're honest. The evidence is adding up to irrefutable levels, especially considering how fine-tuned the universe is for everything to orbit, function, and exist in the way it does. The atheist scientist is being tested like never before.

The odds of a random explosion creating the remarkably detailed outcome that it has is just too complex to be statistically possible. And of course, this is bad news for any atheist. But there's other interesting evidence on a different plane as well.

Hugh Ross, a Christian astrophysicist from the California Institute of Technology, stated that the account of creation as stated in the book of Genesis (at least three thousand years old) is stated in the exact order that things would have had to have occurred. We've been told that the Bible is not a scientific document. Sounds like it might be more than we realize.

Another statement in the book of Job (26:7), in the Old Testament, tells us that the earth is hung in space upon nothing, and therefore not connected to any other object or platform in space. This may sound silly to us today, but it was believed just a few hundred years ago that the earth could not simply be floating in space; it was wildly assumed to be supported by some other object. And Job also told us in verse 37:12 that the earth is round, thousands of years before anyone understood or would believe that to be the case.

For these reasons and many more, some believe modern science to be the enemy of faith, denying what the Bible itself stated thousands of years ago. Not every scientist is an atheist, of course, but the two ways of thinking tend to clash in their ideals. And as we can see from the paragraph above, even "modern science" is sometimes thousands of years behind the Word of God in what it reveals. Ironically, however, all that we're discovering in the cosmos in recent years is increasingly serving to reveal God's existence.

The argument put forth that the universe somehow chaotically burst into existence on its own accord is looking less and less credible, even silly. After all, doesn't it make sense that the thing God created should in fact reveal Him as opposed to hide Him? And another question comes to mind: Can one part of creation—us mere humans—somehow be able to fully explain another part of creation, such as the universe itself? Simple logic is abandoned by otherwise intelligent men, until you bring in the Creator as part of the paradigm of how things came into being.

This has been the folly of an atheistic philosophy all along. It tries to take something God created, and then use it as evidence to deny His existence.

Nonetheless, the atheist continues to work very hard to discredit the existence of God. To their surprise, however, the opposite is happening right before everyone's eyes. Increasing numbers of atheists are being forced to admit that intelligent design simply must be involved in creation. The harder they work to discredit Him, the more they reveal Him. In these last days, God seems to be revealing himself just as much through our understanding of the cosmos as anything else.

For any scientist to deny that the universe was created by intelligent design or a Creator has to take a huge leap of faith, but it's faith in reverse. Faith is a gift from our Creator that we might believe in Him, even if we think the evidence is lacking. But the atheist uses this ability to have faith to *not* believe, even if it denies a plethora of evidence, or the source of that faith. Sadly, it's a chosen delusion, chosen because they don't *want* to believe there is a God. For the believer, however, it's an amazing time to be alive.

Hawking Dies

In the months and years before his death, Hawking seemed increasingly open to the idea of intelligent design and the existence of God outside mere laws of the universe. Could it be that the poster child of secular cosmology secretly became a believer along the way, and chose to reveal this just months before his death? I don't know, but I do know he was honest enough to admit what was becoming irrefutable: that some form of intelligent design had to be behind our remarkable universe. There is simply no other viable possibility, regardless of what someone may hope to be true.

The link between scientific and creationist thought is drawing ever closer. Someday, when the sky rolls back like a scroll and we see all things as they are, we'll find them in perfect harmony. In the end, no argument, philosophy, religion, or scientific hypothesis will keep the truth of God from being revealed— especially His great love for His creation and those who put their trust in Him.

Keep looking up—there's a love letter written in the stars, waiting to be read by you.

Reflection Questions

When you think about the irrefutable message of our universe being proof of intelligent design, how does it affect your own faith in the Creator?

Do you feel the Creator is being generous in revealing so much evidence of His existence, and making it easier than ever to believe in Him? Why or why not?

How might believers share these amazing discoveries about the universe with others, especially unbelievers?

Chapter 9

THE BACKDROP FOR LOVE

*T*he day stood in ordinary form, perfect for a morning jog. With wife and child already back in the United States, Ronnie Smith ran through the streets of Benghazi, Libya with exuberance, perhaps knowing he would soon join his family in the place he called home. All was well and planned well—until a black jeep rolled up beside him.

Ronnie loved God and his family deeply, and leaped at the chance to take that love to the people of Libya. He was honored to share the hope we have in Jesus, and desperately wanted the citizens of Libya to know his Savior's compassion and mercy. Ronnie was well prepared to demonstrate this love while surrounded by those who were hostile to him, and to Christianity itself.

Ronnie received a master's degree in chemistry in 2006 from the University of Texas. His love for teaching brought him and his family to the war-torn country just after its most recent revolution. While there, he desired to radiate the light of God everywhere he went, and to share the goodness of his loving God. Even though Libya is primarily Muslim, Ronnie and his wife Anita were undeterred.

Ronnie considered himself "Libya's best friend" as he shared the gospel of Jesus Christ. But at a cost. While taking his jog on a Thursday morning in December of 2013, a group of men gunned Ronnie down, leaving him for dead on the very streets on which he shared God's amazing love.

A Counterintuitive Love

As barbaric as the slaying of Ronnie Smith was, there's something else that came out of this tragedy that was equally surprising: his wife's response.

Most of us would expect nothing less than anger, a call for justice perhaps, and maybe even revenge against Ronnie's killers. Anita Smith, however, surprised millions by taking a rather unworldly stance.

In an interview with Anderson Cooper of CNN, Anita expressed her love and forgiveness for her husband's killers. "I just really want them to know that I do love them and forgive them,"[6] she stated with a tone of grace. Cooper seemed incredulous that Anita was not filled with some sense of malice toward the shooters. He kept coming back to this point, trying to draw out some sense of abhorrence toward the very people who cut his life short. But Anita kept coming back to how Jesus loves and forgives, and she was going to embody that love no matter what. She expressed pain at the loss of her husband, which was apparent for all to see, but no sign of anger or hostility toward those who murdered Ronnie.

As I researched the details of Ronnie's murder and the unusual response from his wife, there seemed to be a disconnect at first. Who among us wouldn't want justice for anyone who murdered the love of our life, the mother or father of our children? Should not a sin like this be punished? Has love and forgiveness finally gone too far?

One way or another, and perhaps over the course of time, these men will be brought to justice, as they should be. That said, I slowly began to see that sometimes there's a greater cause than justice in the streets—and maybe it's the need to showcase the nature that is God's love, and the remarkably forgiving aspect of that love.

This world has a lot of wrongdoing in it, and the wheels of justice are constantly turning to address those wrongs. What the world needs more of, however, is extravagant examples of the ultimate solution for all the world's and its people's ills: God's love and mercy.

In Anita's interview, love and forgiveness were at center stage, not the terrible crime or what kind of people would carry out such a deed. Anita seemed to leave those issues in God's hands. As for her hands and her heart, they would be about love and forgiveness as a source of the healing our world needs. The situation served as a reminder that a godly love sometimes stands out best amidst the background of a dark and violent world.

Darkness Remains

The darkness in this world is alarming, and increasingly so. The escalation of unchecked criminality alone makes one wonder where we're headed as a civilized society, both here in the US and abroad. Criminality and wrongdoing has to be addressed as needed; God's love does not negate that fact. If we don't address it, all that's left is chaos and tyranny.

We often hear that this world is not supposed to be this way, as if all things have slipped from God's hands and his will, and that the world is supposed to be different. God's Word, however, suggests a different reality.

Scripture tells us that humans have purposely been set in the midst of both good and evil for a time, and I believe that's been the plan all along. The friction this causes everyone makes for a difficult life, to be sure, but it serves its purpose. In fact, God's Word is clear that the Creator leaves evil in place for the purpose of training his people, delivering the wrongdoer to justice, and bringing out the best in godly people over time. This process will ultimately cause the righteous to shine, and also bring due glory to our great and loving God.

Another part of that end goal is that we may put both good and evil into right perspective: to learn to love what is right, holy, and true—and in addition, to hate what is false, vile, and spiritually dark. But in our world, the lines between good and evil get easily blurred.

We humans easily struggle to separate truth from the lie, good from bad. We get our emotions, motives, personal preferences, and a myriad of thoughts so entangled that we easily get confused concerning what is right versus wrong. In American culture today, this has never been truer. But when our loving God pits evil and good against each other, and sometimes in very stark terms, it has a way of clearing up our fuzzy outlook and giving us real clarity.

We may not like the fact that evil remains in the world, and may even think it unnecessary. Many don't see the point. But when I think of all the ways in which God uses evil to sharpen our gaze, and how God has used it in my own life, I can't help but wonder if the primary reason is that we simply couldn't see the light, truth, and love without it. Without the daily displays of selfishness, and sometimes the brutal and despicable behavior of some, we may not fully appreciate the gentleness and love of a holy God. The two are constantly being lived out right before our eyes, which necessarily creates a much needed contrast between them.

God Is Proactive

I used to think that as evil increases, God responds by countering it with more truth. I eventually realized, however, that this philosophy is reactionary at best. What if the opposite is true? Perhaps as truth and love increase, evil responds in an effort to snuff out God's light with chaos, division, and clear undermining of what's holy, right, and true. As I look around, I see that the love, goodness, and grace of God abounds in our world every day, in one form or another.

And while we need to address the wrong and not turn a blind eye to its reality, we can't let it become such a distraction that we fail to see the good all around. When it becomes a distraction, that's when we lose perspective. Which, in turn, could be a clever effort to rob us of the great work God is doing in this world—especially His great love that is all around us, and in so many wonderful people.

One of those great people is Anita Smith, whose interview on CNN demonstrated a heart devoted to the love and goodness of God. and was a powerful witness to just how far-reaching God's love is. Her interview pierced me in a way no planned speech or charismatic preacher could have. One could not simply arrange such effectiveness to the love and mercy of God.

But real love, set in a dark world as its background, can.

Reflection Questions

How do you feel about living in a world in which there is pain and suffering, and yet so much love and goodness as well?

Can you think of some examples in which God's love shines best amidst a dark and nasty world?

Are there some areas in which you personally have experienced God's love and kindness because of something negative that happened in your life?

Chapter 10

POWER IN CONSTRAINT

Morning's dawn had yet to appear. The night owl still sat proudly upon his perch. And the morning dew had yet to sparkle under the sun's early light. I rose early that morning with the intention of reading alone, and to enjoy the silence of a house still under sleep's faithful spell. My only companions were burning logs in the fireplace and the book I was about to read. As I began to flip through its pages, my attention suddenly turned toward the fire itself. I was captured by its soft glow. Its gentle heat. And the nearly hypnotic comfort it provided on this winter morning. As I stared into its colorful flames, my mind shifted again, but this time toward the fire's enormous power.

I then pondered the fact that as long as the fire is contained, it remains my friend. Uncontained, however, it can destroy all I love in a matter of hours, even minutes. One spark thrust outside set perimeters can alter the course of one's life forever, and with not a hint of mercy.

In recent history, entire towns have been leveled by the unquenched momentum of raging flames. In Australia in 2019, the worst fires on record destroyed much of its vast tropical rainforest.

On this morning, however, with its given constraints, the fire could only do good.

Fire's Power

The collection of firepower, or weaponry, which the world's largest nations hold in their arsenal represents an alarming power. Should Russia, China, and the United States ever decide to duke it out, enormous destruction and death would occur. The constraint shown by these superpowers, however, render these weapons as mere tools of political sway, and as bargaining chips that may ironically help to avert war. For now, they are mere bloviations of force.

In addition, the same nuclear power that killed hundreds of thousands of Japanese with the atom bomb during World War II also provides electricity for heating and cooling homes for millions worldwide, including the United States. Interest in nuclear power remains tepid, however—partially because of costs, but also because of the possibility of nuclear accidents like those at Three Mile Island, Chernobyl, and most recently the Fukushima Daiichi nuclear disaster. Nuclear power can do much good. Unconstrained, however, its destructive powers are potentially catastrophic.

Many countries are tempted by nuclear firepower, and will risk starving their own people in an effort to attain it. The temptation is too great, regardless of the enormous political and financial price they pay. Once unconstrained, however—or worse, weaponized—it could very well bring an end to the world as we know it.

The power held within our universe, however, makes fire, conventional weaponry, and even nuclear power look minuscule by comparison. It is estimated that just one gamma-ray burst throughout the universe will emit more energy in seconds than our sun will in ten billion years.

The Creator's Power

As awe-inspiring as these powers are, someone had to create them. And it stands to reason that the Creator's power would exceed anything creation itself could demonstrate. From the One who created fire, nuclear power, and gamma rays lies the ability to destroy them by a simple command. And why not? His very words spoke all things into existence; certainly He can speak them out of existence. His own power is superior to all that creation contains.

What moves me the most, however, is not God's incomprehensible power, but rather His remarkable constraint in using it.

Power Driven by Love

This controlled power allows a tiny planet called Earth to harbor oxygen, to hold water to its surface, and to compel a gentle breeze to cool one's skin on a hot day. It allows an enduring atmosphere to blanket the earth as protection from the harshness of space, and to allow the most tender part of creation to thrive. Earth is the only habitable place for humans in all of space that we know of. Even with our relatively mild weather variations, Earth is mostly a gentle and livable environment. And it took great power to make it so.

The deeper we look into space, the more desolation we find. Only vast wastelands on other planets, though were assured by some that there's other worlds out there just like our own. The more we look, however, the more we confirm this not to be true.

When astronauts return from space, they speak of the pleasure of having had the chance to get a closer look at other planets. But their deepest affection is sometimes reserved for the tiny blue planet they call home: Earth. Some astronauts are moved nearly to tears as they gaze upon Earth's welcoming blue-and-white appearance set amidst the blackness of space. Sitting in a small spacecraft, soaring through space at upward of twenty thousand miles per hour, they speak of their yearning to come back to the one planet on which they were designed to live and thrive. From the great void of space, Earth never looks more appealing.

What great and intentional power it took to create our magnificent Earth, to establish its majesty among all the other heavenly bodies, and to set it securely upon its rightful throne. What great power it took to fine-tune its position and suspend its mass in space, and to maintain that position for millennia or longer—just so we may breathe its oxygen, bask in its warm sun, drink its water, and eat its food. That we may live our lives, pursue our passions, and experience life by the generous hand of a benevolent God. And all perfectly orchestrated that you and I may smile at a stunning sunrise, ponder the hidden message within a breathtaking sunset, and long to know the One who imagined it all, who created it all.

Our world forged in great power is what allows a raindrop to feed the ground, a flower to grow, and a snowflake to form just under the right conditions. Under God's constrained power a fawn is born in the wild, a bird is fed by its mother, and a nest for her offspring is held together only by tiny sticks and natural debris.

The smallest spiders and creatures crawl about the earth's surface, barely seen with the naked eye, and yet are given the morning dew for drink and the smallest of particles for food. The Word of God tells us there is not a single creature on the earth, neither great or small, that God is not aware of. He feeds them all, delights in their existence, and has created the perfect ecosystem for their survival. God loves His creation.

The slightest adjustment to the cosmos, the most minute change in the earth's position on its invisible axis, or the most detailed modification to the earth's proximity to the sun, and Earth would become another wasteland. As God's power is constrained, it's also maintained to unimaginable specificity, all the while remaining fragile—entirely for our survival, intentionally for our pleasure, and hopefully that we may know His love.

When Jesus walked the earth and was abused at the hands of his enemies, a massive army of powerful angels were at his disposal should he choose to fight back. The prophet Isaiah (37:36) describes an event at which one angel destroyed 185,000 men in one night. This kind of power was at Jesus's disposal. He chose, however, to constrain such power—and to be profoundly disrespected, beaten, tortured, and finally killed upon the cross. He subdued the enormous power at His disposal for only one reason: that we may know His love.

Power to Force

This level of constraint can only come from a God who loves his children more than His own power. From this place of uncompromised commitment to His offspring, His tenderness, kindness, and compassion come forth so that He might protect all He holds dear, and to win our hearts in the process.

He has all the power in the world to force us to obey, to coerce anyone and anything into submission, and to perform just as He wishes. And if He did, He would remain sovereign. But He's not like us humans, who use power only to control and manipulate. Rather, He prefers to nudge with a whisper, to delight with wonderful displays of creation, to cast hints of His love through the fragrance of springtime or the sunlight glistening on tree leaves just after a rain. He would rather woo you with a sunset than force you with His undeniable power.

His influence is subtle persuasion, though He can be resisted. He stirs the heart with tenderness, invites all to the landscape of a soft heart, though hearts may choose to remain hard. He moves us with His own humility, though we can respond with pride. All this risk, however, is intended to give us room to choose Him freely, at the risk of being rejected. Those are the stakes of love, even for God.

All the while the world mocks the name of Jesus our God, takes his name in vain without a blush, and rejects His many offerings. In my own country, the United States, we seem to be slowly raising our noses and tilting our brows at His gentle beckoning and His humble call.

I don't know about you, but I can trust my life to a God who's willing to constrain such remarkable power for a little while and use it only for good—all that I may know His faithful love.

What great respect our Creator has for His children, that we may use our freedom to not only accept his love but even to discard it. A God who's willing to pacify His power for a time, so that we may choose to trust Him and give Him our all. What human would humble him or herself to this degree, and for the sake of selfless love?

I'm little persuaded by religion or what others say or believe. But I am moved deeply by a loving God such as ours who is filled with such remarkable kindness, abundant mercy, and wholehearted acceptance toward anyone who will simply turn to Him.

Reflection Questions

How do you feel about God's love not being forceful, but giving us all room to trust in that love?

Can you think of some subtle examples of how God's love calls your name?

What situations really stand out in terms of God's love being shown to you, or coming to light?

What does this make you want to tell others in regard to God's love for a hurting world?

Chapter 11

WHAT A FATHER WANTS

*A*s we continue exploring the various ways God demonstrates His love amidst a dark and flawed world, the emphasis is primarily placed on what God does for us. After all, as we seek God, we are promised forgiveness for our sins, favor in every part of life, and peace in times of trouble. What God wants *from* us, however, is another matter, and one rarely spoken of. In fact, what our God desires in return for His love may reveal more about His heart than anything else.

Have you ever wondered what God wants from His children in general, or from you personally? Do you ever consider what kind of relationship God is looking for, and what all that might entail? I've wondered this myself, along with what brings God joy. God's Word reveals that He's capable of feeling both joy and pain. Believe it or not, how we live our lives and whether or not we're willing to interact with Him can bring either one to our heavenly Father.

In faith and religion, God's expectations for us mean different things to different people. And our own interpretation may depend on how we were raised, in what light God was presented to us early in life, along with a thousand other influences. Some believe that God wants them to have blind obedience for Him, sometimes at the expense of innate hopes or dreams. Others just want a list of rules to follow and nothing else.

Others still view their walk strictly in terms of going to church on Sunday morning; what they do or how they live their life the other six days is a different matter. Sadly, I've met many people who view their walk in this fashion as they try and live out two different personas altogether. And yet others feel that what God wants from them is to live a life that never fails or falters. This idealistic group easily gets caught in the delusion of not making any mistakes and being "perfect Christians." But when they inevitably stumble, shame fills them as they view themselves as failures, letting themselves, their congregations, and God Himself down.

Finally, some believe that what God wants from them is a constant involvement in a faith-based charity or a noble work of some kind, even if they keep their hearts from God and their own family in the process. I see some who sacrifice relational quality with their families and God, and are worn out as a result.

While I have certainly been immersed in some of the above mindsets in the past, my perspective changed dramatically when I became a father.

A Father's Perspective

As our first daughter came into the world, I was unprepared for the level of joy that would fill my being. As I laid my eyes on her for the first time, the miracle of her creation and birth overwhelmed me in a way I didn't expect. Waves of gratitude rushed my soul and my joy had never felt more complete. As a result, a new purpose for existing was also born that day. I was introduced to a different kind of love: a father's love.

I have come to realize that one of the best teachers about the heart of our God is becoming parents ourselves. The moment we do, we instantly share something in common with the Creator of the Universe: we both now have children. We find ourselves unable to stop staring at this little human being of whom we took part in creating. And as we take on this new role with a dedicated spirit of love and responsibility; it weighs on us like nothing else.

If I, a mere man, can feel that for my daughter, how much more does the holy God of love feel that way about you and me? He's the real Creator. We're His offspring. We can only imagine loving from God's perspective. But as a father, I begin to understand as I see more of the heart of God.

But lately I've been thinking about what we want *from* our children. That may sound off-base, even wrongheaded. We are there to serve, nurture, and love our children. But as they grow and mature, at some point most of us want the relationship to become reciprocal. I mean, isn't that the goal? This is where the things a father wants, including our heavenly Father, begin to come into a clearer view.

Hope in a Response

One day while working in my home office, one of my daughters gently pushed my door open and tenderly stated that she had made something for me, and that she wanted to give it to me. She must have been 3 or 4 at the time. As she brought me this simple drawing she had created with me in mind, I knew in that moment that our relationship had become reciprocal. I didn't expect it to happen this early. In her own way she was returning some of the love I had been giving to her. The moment was so precious to me, so pure and innocent, that it nearly moved me to tears. Her simple gesture engaged my heart in a way only a parent could understand.

She was not prompted to do this, of course; it was entirely of her own volition. And I knew that love was coming back my way, and that our relationship had just gone to a new level: the level of mutual love.

Of Her Own Volition

Imagine for a moment that I had arranged for my little girl to come into my office that day and give me a gift, or that I had established a rule in our house that our kids had to produce so many drawings each week and provide so many gifts, and that there were a certain number of hugs that had to be given, along with the requirement to say "I love you" so many times a day. Or, that there was one day of the week that they were told to focus on me more than the other six days of the week and that any hopes, dreams, or desires had to be sacrificed for their relationship with me. If we wouldn't want that as human parents, why would our father in heaven want that?

We must teach our kids to live within certain guidelines, obey certain rules, and place upon them various expectations, all for their safety and ability to thrive in life. But you can't do that with what matters most: love, affection and loyalty—not if you want any kind of a valuable relationship. It must come from the heart, and of one's own choosing. We can demonstrate this to our children by how we treat them. But until they freely offer it back, and spontaneously, it remains a one-way relationship.

No matter how perfectly our children carry out a command for the sake of the command, it would always lack the free will to simply return the love we had been giving to them. Even a good deed means very little if obligation is involved in the slightest. A gift cannot be demanded or forced, and still remain a gift. At that point, it becomes a payment. If obligation of any kind is involved, it would not be giving at all.

But this is what Christianity has become for many: a payment paid instead of a gift given. This is not only true in the realm of giving money, but in giving our entire selves to our Creator, just because we want a real connection with Him. Just because we love Him. So many today seem to be looking for relationships of mere transaction—relationships in which they can get something from others, not just for the sake of being friends or being there for someone.

Our God is not like that, however. Yes, our lives are to bring glory to Him. But He's not a glory hound like some paint Him to be. He's a God who desires a mutual relationship with His children. And I believe this to be the primary reason He created humanity.

The Heart of God

Some of you might say to me, "Preston, we're human, and God is God. Your comparison isn't valid." Here's the truth, though: we're made in the image of God. The general pattern of who God is happens to be written on our hearts and minds more accurately than any other being. God cannot have this type of relationship with the angels, or any other creatures He's created. Therefore, the relationship between human parent and child serves as a very accurate analogy to our relationship with our heavenly Father. Why do you think the family unit, as humanity has known it for thousands of years, is coming under attack the way it is? Because it reveals the heart of God. The enemy will do anything to hide the heart of God from unsuspecting people.

Nothing moves me more than when one of my girls comes to me with something that gives them great joy, really moves them, or has caused great pain for them in some way. The fact that they trust me enough to bring their tender hearts to me in a moment of vulnerability means a lot. To earn their trust in such a tender moment is precious beyond words. If you're a parent, you know what this is like. Yet I must acknowledge that my heart came from God. He created it and molded it to reflect *His* heart. So, my experience tells me much about what our loving God is like, and the way He loves.

I believe that this is the kind of connection God desires with you and me. Our wonderful God longs for nothing more than for you to come to Him willingly—to lay out what's on your mind and heart, including any fears, hurts, longings and dreams. God considers these moments precious, because you're revealing the very contents of your being, and in faith trusting Him with whatever you share. This is cherished by God more than anything. Anything!

Our Gift to God

I don't draw pictures for God; He's the One who paints sunsets. I don't buy him anything, He owns everything from the diamond mines of Africa to the gold mines of Alaska. I don't perform empty religious rituals for Him, for He can make stones cry out and worship Him. But I do practice giving him what I believe He wants the most: my whole heart, and everything it consists of, including —my hopes, dreams, desires, pain, concerns about our world, even what angers me. When I do, a mutual relationship happens. Love happens. There is simply nothing better.

And when God answers me, He answers in no uncertain terms. Not out loud, but with a new perspective. A fresh point of view. A happier spirit. A lighter load. And it is here that I have found life. Freedom. Healing. And best of all, His faithful love.

Whatever our purpose in life is, it begins by being real before the One who made us, hiding nothing. Give this to God, and you give Him the treasure of His heart: an authentic and trusted connection with you, His precious child.

What's in my heart isn't always pretty, and that may be the case with you. But God is merciful and forgiving. He's not looking for perfection; he's looking for honesty, transparency, and authenticity. Don't we want the same in our relationship with others? If we're willing to face our own darkness inside, He'll face it with us. And He'll cleanse us as truly only He can.

The Grip of Bitterness

Some Christians, however, are angry with God, and have found other ways of resisting Him. If that is you, I know what that feels like. I've been there. My early years were plagued with anger for a variety of reasons. But we must understand that God is not the problem—He's the solution. Tell God why you are angry. Why you hurt. Why you're afraid. But don't stop there: ask Him to help you deal with whatever's going on and whatever you've been through. If I hadn't done that in my own life, I'd be in serious trouble now.

It may be someone else's fault; it may be your own fault. Either way, He's a healer. A forgiver. A problem-solver. A way-maker. The point is to lay all at His feet. He can take it. He's a strong God. He is looking for a reciprocal relationship, a mutual friendship, one based in the reality of who we really are and what we're really struggling with. And that requires honesty in both directions, does it not?

Our God isn't interested in phony religious activity. Wearing ourselves out through works. Pouring our entire being into a congregation or hanging on every word our pastor says. There's an appropriate application for all of these. But He primarily desires that our foundation and strength come first from abiding in Him—by maintaining a real and honest connection with a real

God, our God and Savior Christ Jesus. Christianity is not a religion; it's a person.

God made us for a relationship based in love. And given how much that love benefits us, don't we "owe" God a genuine love in return? Maybe it's time you push His door open and give Him something you've prepared for Him—namely, your whole heart. He is your Creator, after all. He's given you life and all that it entails.

That's the way He loves.

Reflection Questions

What is your impression of God, knowing that He doesn't want a religious or a legalistic relationship with us, but rather a reciprocal relationship of mutual love?

How would you describe your own connection with the God of love?

Have there been any distractions or impediments to that connection? If so, what are they?

How would you describe a healthy relationship with your Creator, and what do you long for the most in your connection with Jesus, the God of true love?

Chapter 12

GREATER TO BE KNOWN

*T*he technology we have through the Hubble Telescope and gravity wave telescopes are allowing us to see deeper into space than ever before. That includes the ability to observe small distortions of space/time, as predicted by Albert Einstein's theory of general relativity. They were launched into space years ago and have sent back thousands of pictures at which to marvel. We now know what we once thought were bright stars far away are entire galaxies, some of which can be seen with the naked eye. And the number of galaxies in the entire universe is currently estimated to be about two trillion. Yes, two trillion galaxies. It truly boggles the mind.

These modern telescopes allow us to see objects as far away as thirty billion light years, even though the universe itself is "only" about thirteen billion years old. This is true because the farther away a galaxy is, the faster it is expanding away from us, therefore increasing its distance beyond the age of the universe itself. Try and wrap your mind around that.

The amazing photos these telescopes are taking may suggest these galaxies are closer than they appear, or that they are within reach for space travel. But the truth about the expanse of the cosmos is hard to fathom. Without math, we would have no method for describing its size in any real terms. Even if we could travel at the speed of light (186,792 miles/299,792 kilometers per second) it would still take us billions of years to reach many of the deep space galaxies. How great is our God who created such an enormous universe.

Our Own Galaxy

With our ability to view deep space with its stunning celestial bodies so far away, and with the most advanced telescopes ever created, there's an irony that should be pointed out: we are unable to view or take any pictures of the galaxy that our earth sits right in the middle of, the Milky Way Galaxy.

Because Earth is in its midst, we can only estimate the Milky Way Galaxy's size, its outer boundaries, and what it may look like from a distance; experts estimate it to be 150,000 to 200,000 light years across. We aren't even certain where Earth sits within the Milky Way, although it's estimated to be somewhere within one of its outer rings. Few other details about the Milky Way Galaxy, and Earth's proximity to it are known, especially compared to other galaxies we observe much farther out in space.

In order to get a good look, we'd have to travel at the speed of light for about 20,000 years to just get out of our own galaxy, and then another 20,000 years or so just to get far enough away to take a picture of the Milky Way Galaxy in one frame. And that may not even be far enough. If Adam and Eve had stepped into a spaceship the day they were kicked out of Eden and began traveling at the speed of light, they would not have even left our own galaxy yet. The fact is, we're simply too close to our own galaxy to see it for what it is.

As people, we have the exact same problems in trying to view or understand ourselves, and for the same reasons.

Know Thyself

I don't have to tell you that we live in a very self-focused society. Increasingly, we're called to "know thyself." We put great effort into specifying our own preferences, likes, dislikes, desires, wants and so on. If there ever were a "me" generation, it is us today. We almost never hear the call to know and understand *others* better.

But even with a healthy sense of self-reflection and the need to know who we are on some level, can we really achieve this with any sense of accuracy or objectivity? And if we can't, does any other human being have that capability? I don't think so.

Truly, there's only one who can. And we're in desperate need of His personal assessment of the truest parts of our inner person.

Being Known

Our Creator sees us from beginning to end: the whole of our existence, and with 100% truth and objectivity. After all, He carefully handcrafted every one of us to His liking. And God's Word says He sees our whole lives all at once because He's not limited by the chronology of time like we are, or its impending decay. For Him, this is not complex, not a mystery. Who we are, what we'll become, and what we're capable of is only known by the one who made us. And this is an important truth for a myriad of reasons.

As we are incapable of seeing ourselves with any true sense of objectivity and know that another human being cannot either, we only have our Creator to look to. Therefore, our only hope is that we allow our God to take up residence inside. But why is this so crucial?

When assessing our inner person, God must consider not only what we're capable of in this life but also in the life to come. It's what we *would* do if we were given unlimited power that is of great concern to our God. Throughout our lives, we all perform small acts of good and evil. Neither may affect the world around us with any measurable effect. But if we were given infinite power, each of us could do either exponentially great good or great harm in the eternal realm. Only God knows our true capacity—what we are capable of ultimately. So, we're wise to trust Him with our whole being, and not rely on our own self-assessment.

A King Who Sought to Be Known

One man in history valued the need to be known by God perhaps as well as anyone: King David. He once wrote: "Search me, God, and know my heart; test me and know my anxious thoughts" (Psalm 139:23). David learned early in life that his heart was capable of some dark deeds. Once he saw the sin for what it was, however, it horrified him and he repented fully. In time, David learned how crucial it was that God was allowed into His heart, to search its chambers and to clean it up. He wanted to know God, but he understood that it was far more important that God knew him, and knew every part of his being.

Maybe we learn 1 percent of who and what God is during this life. I don't know. But God knows 100 percent of our being, even before we are born. That fact should give us pause.

For he chose us in him before the creation of the world to be holy and blameless in his sight. (Ephesians 1:4)

We are a universe of thoughts, desires, and motives that have eternal implications, in which both good and evil can be carried out with ongoing impact—an impact that could cause a ripple effect through the bandwidth of time. When we ask God to know us, we're asking the Almighty to make sure that only good is present, and to rid our hearts of the slightest evil. If the tiniest blemish of evil remains in our hearts, great evil could arise from it.

This can only happen if we let God know our innermost thoughts, both good and bad. He's made it clear that He will not force His way in. He is a gentle and loving God, and wants us to have say in the matter. We have the power to keep God out of our hearts, and prevent Him from truly knowing us in the way He desires. I've watched too many people do this until the day of their death. In truth, they lose everything. Keeping God at a distance, the only one who can really change their hearts, has both tragic repercussions and eternal implications.

As we put our faith in Christ our Savior, we must do everything in our power to allow Him in, even the dark places. Places of shame. The places of our pain. We must give Him permission to perform the heart surgery we are all in desperate need of. When we do, that's when healing begins.

We're Too Close

As humans, we seek to know things. To know a skill or a craft. To know people. We seek knowledge because we want to know some smart and good things. Most of us want to be "in the know." But it's better to be known.

The focus of knowing only ourselves is wracked with the potential of narcissism, self-obsession, and even delusion. Why? Because we're in the middle of our own galaxy. We're too close to the complex universe that is our mind and heart to see it for what it is. And we can't get far enough away from ourselves to see ourselves objectively. We'll always be biased toward the self. Therefore, nothing is more important, more valuable, and more accurate than God's assessment of who we are. Notice Jesus's words below:

> Many will say to me on [judgment day], "Lord, Lord, did we not prophesy in your name and in your name drive out demons and, in your name, perform many miracles?" Then I will tell them plainly, "I never knew you. Away from me, you evildoers!" (Matthew 7:22–23)

As wonderful as the universe is, you are His favorite part of creation. But we must respond to His love, let Him in, and hide nothing from Him. After all, He created everything, so that you and I may know His love.

> [W]hoever loves God is known by God.
> (1 Corinthians 8:3)

Reflection Questions

Does it surprise you that it's more important to be known by God? Explain.

Do you feel you have an open and transparent relationship with God? Explain.

Is there anything in your heart or mind you have yet to take to your Father in prayer? If so, what?

What have been the results of either keeping something from your heavenly Father, or of trusting everything to God?

Chapter 13

THE SHREWD FATHER

I have always found our God to be merciful, patient, and generous. In forty years of abiding under the cover of his faithfulness, He has never failed me. But there's another side to the nature of God I've come to know and respect: His shrewdness.

"Shrewd" may be thought of as being extremely detailed in one's dealings with others, or clever in their approach. We may associate this term with a hard-dealing businessman or a highly skilled negotiator. Because of this, the idea of a loving God being shrewd may seem contradictory or even ungodly, especially in an age where many use their shrewdness for selfish gain or greedy pursuits. Regarding our God, however, this could not be further from the truth.

Let's take a closer look at how the "shrewd" side of the Creator not only is used in holy ways, but is highly beneficial to those who trust Him. We will also learn how effective shrewdness is in dealing with the wicked.

The Need for Shrewd

Our God is filled with love and mercy, especially for those who seek him with a pure heart. But for those who are seeking otherwise, they will meet a shrewd God. King David said this about God's nature: "to the pure you show yourself pure, but to the devious you show yourself shrewd" (Psalm 18:26)

God holds compassion for the brokenhearted, especially for those willing to call on Him for help. But when Jesus walked the earth, He showed decisive shrewdness toward the religious who oppressed the poor and loved their own animals more than other people. On one occasion he stated bluntly, "You snakes! You brood of vipers! How will you escape being condemned to hell?" (Matthew 23:33).

Once, while in a boat with his disciples, a storm arose, and the wind and waves grew in passion. But Jesus simply stated, "Quiet! Be still!" and the winds and waves fell into passive calm (Mark 4:39). On another occasion, however, he condemned a bush along the side of the road for not producing fruit, stating that it would never produce fruit again (Matthew 21:19). This bush didn't find God's grace, but it did encounter decisive shrewdness from its Creator.

Jesus demonstrated profound compassion toward those who doubted Him, such as Thomas, and no doubt many others. But He turned with sharp rebuke toward those who rejected Him outright. It may appear that Jesus was being contradictory or inconsistent in His approach. In reality, however, he was simply being shrewd. He knew who belonged to Him and who didn't.

This trait may not give us the warm and fuzzies about God, but it does remind us that we're being protected by the most brilliant being in the universe, and that no one can outsmart Him. If we think we can negotiate certain sinful behavior into approval, we must think again. As God's Word reminds us, "Do not be deceived: God cannot be mocked. A man reaps what he sows" (Galatians 6:7). Ouch! Clearly God shows no favoritism, even though some are hoping He'll turn a blind eye come Judgment Day. But that's simply not the picture the Bible paints of God. He's too shrewd to be taken advantage of by anyone, including the brightest among us.

The shrewd nature of God does raise a question, however: Is God ever shrewd in dealing with his own people, or just toward the wicked? Well, both, but in different ways. In fact, I believe this to be one of the most misunderstood aspects of our God and the nature of Jesus. We tend to either see Him as cold and distant, seemingly unknowable, or as passive and permissive, allowing pretty much anything in the name of grace. Though I believe the masses fall into either one or the other philosophy, they both fail to see the more complex Creator that Scripture reveals.

God's Shrewdness with His People

We just looked at how God is shrewd with the wicked. But what about His people? God is shrewd with us, but in a different way than with those who hate Him. If that sounds inappropriate, or ill-fit for how we normally think of God, stay with me here. For the shrewd nature must be in the mix for God to be effective in our lives, especially if we're to mature in faith and better learn to walk closely with Him. Not everyone is comfortable with this side of the Creator, and may even recoil at the thought of it. But the truth is, we *need* God to be shrewd.

What may appear to be contradictory to us is sometimes a parallel truth that runs alongside another truth. God's shrewdness is one of those corresponding truths. It allows Him to be loving and filled with grace, while also working on our hearts with detail and shrewdness. We must be willing to look at God's multifaceted nature if we're to better know Him, His will in our lives, and His amazing love for us. This is part of understanding God's nature, along with the story of God and humanity.

A Return on Investment

The story of God and humanity is the greatest story of all time. It's a profound and historic story about how a good God created His offspring for the purpose of sharing His love, and then desiring that we reciprocate that love. But humanity rejected that holy and generous love and turned toward evil instead.

However, because God is holy, right, and true, He cannot compromise his very own nature of truth. The sin of rejecting God had to be recompensed for, atoned for in some way, even punished. Therefore God sent Jesus, His only Son, to die for us and to atone for sin on our behalf—and in the process, redeem us back to Him. Nothing we ever teach or say should ever contradict that splendid truth, nor the great love shown us in this sacrificial act of love from the Father.

Part of this story however is that through the suffering and death of Christ Jesus, God has made a tremendous investment in His people, and the process of redemption. Perhaps we'll never fully understand the level of sacrifice and the pain God endured, all to save you and me.

But knowing that God is shrewd, He's going to make sure He gets a return on His investment. He's purchased us, after all, and with the blood of His own Son, Jesus the Christ. The price was high, the suffering immense. Therefore, we must understand that God's going to profit from all He's invested in us. And it's perfectly appropriate that He does. But how does God profit from us?

The Parable That Reveals God's Shrewdness

The parable of the talents illustrates the shrewd side of God's nature better than any other part of God's Word. I'm going to paraphrase it, but you can read all of it in Matthew 25:14–30.

The parable speaks of three different individuals who were all given various levels of talents, or bags of gold, depending on which gospel or translation you read. And two of them went out and invested their given talent, and then reaped a reward as a result.

One of the recipients, however, was too timid to invest what he had been freely given by the master. This person did nothing with their given talent, and returned what he had to the Creator, and with zero interest or profit. But God's response to the unfruitful person, the person who showed no profit, reveals much about how God views His investment, and His expectations of those He's invested in.

> But his lord answered and said to him, "You wicked and lazy servant, you knew that I reap where I have not sown, and gather where I have not scattered seed. So you ought to have deposited my money with the bankers, and at my coming I would have received back my own with interest. So take the talent from him, and give it to him who has ten talents.
>
> "For to everyone who has, more will be given, and he will have abundance; but from him who does not have, even what he has will be taken away. And cast the unprofitable servant into the outer darkness. There will be weeping and gnashing of teeth." (Matthew 25:26–30, NKJV)

God's Right to Expect a Profit

God doesn't require a high profit, but He requires a profit nonetheless. If we come to the end of our lives and we're exactly the same people with the same flaws and sins as in the beginning, there would be no profit to show. God expects us to overcome sin and abound in the fruits of the Spirit. He has a right to—we're part of the creation He's invested in. Our refusal to grow would be remarkably insulting. Refusing to overcome is tantamount to rejecting the Creator, and that rejection would be the same as embracing evil. There's no way around that fact.

Some criticize God for His response, or for the shrewdness of His insistence on a profit. The truth is, we're exactly the same. If we invest time, money, or emotions in a relationship, a stock, or a hobby, aren't we disappointed, even incredulous, if there's absolutely no return on our investment? Of course we are.

Wouldn't we also say it was a complete waste of time? Don't we eventually reject someone who has made it clear they want nothing to do with us? And yet we're only human. How much more does the holy and righteous Creator have a right to be angry if we reject Him and want nothing to do with Him? For He alone gave us life, and everything in it.

We Need God to Be Shrewd with Us

I personally can say that if God weren't shrewd with me on some things, I would have never been willing to overcome and leave some stuff behind. He's always been gentle and patient—but still shrewd. Whatever He sets out to address with us, He'll address it; you can be sure. By making sure we overcome and become fruitful sons and daughters of God, we are also able to share in his great gifts, opportunities, and authentic joy. That is the fruit of being shrewd. And only then are we authentic witnesses.

If God weren't shrewd in training us, we wouldn't have anything to celebrate come harvest time, both in this age and the age
to come. If not for His insistence that we overcome, and his ability
to outwit our most clever arguments for the flesh, we would never
leave behind an existence that's bound to depravity and keeps us
in shackles.

But it's even better than that. Because God is shrewd, we'll
experience levels of success in every part of our lives. As God pros-
pers from us, we prosper along with Him as He shares the fruit
with us.

I have gone through some tough things that made me question
whether God was really looking out for me. Maybe you have too.
But when the trouble cleared and my peace returned, I could see
that God had equipped me with a new maturity and understanding that better prepared me for future challenges. The truth is,
one cannot really be happy or fruitful in life without God dealing
shrewdly with our otherwise corrupt nature.

> To him who *overcomes* I will give to eat from the tree
> of life, which is in the midst of the Paradise of God.
> (Revelation 2:7, NKJV, emphasis added)

Our Need to Be Shrewd

Jesus tells a story in the Gospel of Luke in which a master's servant
was caught being unproductive and dishonest with his master's
wealth and affairs. He was told to get his house in order because
the master was coming and would deal with him harshly.

Fearing the loss of his livelihood, the servant got busy and
found a way to benefit his master, his master's customers, *and*
himself—and with clever shrewdness. Jesus said this about the
man who went from being lazy, unproductive, and complacent, to

being shrewd: "The master commended the dishonest manager because he had acted *shrewdly*. For the people of this world are more *shrewd* in dealing with their own kind than are the people of the light" (Luke 16:8, emphasis added).

God is not condoning dishonesty here. Jesus is simply complimenting the man for using his head and finding a way to benefit everyone involved. If we are to abound in this life, both for ourselves and others, we must learn a proper form of shrewdness. If you're passive, naïve, and overly sensitive and just expect life to fall into your lap, you'll be disappointed. Worse, you'll accomplish very little, maybe nothing. You'll be of little use to others. So learn to be shrewd—but learn it God's way.

The difference between a shrewd but corrupt businessman and God is that God is holy, loving, and good. He's incapable of defrauding anyone. Therefore, his insistence on a profit (our overcoming sin and producing righteous fruit) is just as much to our benefit as it is God's. This brings great honor to God, and great blessings to us. Remember, God values a reciprocal relationship, and rewards those who engage Him intentionally.

As we profit in God, and overcome past sins, we possess the tools and skills to live well and put down evil in the process. Without the insistence to do so by our Creator, we simply would be ill-equipped to face evil, overcome temptation, and stand for righteousness—all crucial aspects of a successful Christian life. The refusal to do so is the same as refusing God's training and letting evil have its way. There is no middle or neutral ground. That's a trap many fall into, and a fantasy many embrace. We either stand for good or evil. That's the reality. There is no door number three, no matter how much we may love the TV game show *The Price Is Right*.

Stand up and be shrewd toward evil. This is a great gift from God. Don't waste it. As the Word says, "No one can serve two masters. Either you will hate the one and love the other, or you will be devoted to the one and despise the other" (Matthew 6:24).

As a businessman, I would not survive if I were not appropriately shrewd. The business world will eat you alive if you're unprepared in any way. The difference, however, is that I'm a Christian. My type of shrewdness is not unethical, cruel, or sinful. If it were, I would lose my witness and be at odds with my God. I do it with humility, for I'm not anyone's judge. I only walk as one whose many sins have been forgiven.

That said, Christians are never to be anyone's doormat. A proper level of shrewdness will keep you from that false notion. You can be respectful, even loving, and shrewd at the same time. As Jesus said, "I am sending you out like sheep among wolves. Therefore, be as *shrewd* as snakes and as innocent as doves" (Matthew 10:16, emphasis added). God has no intention of raising a feeble and unproductive generation— He's raising the mighty people of God. A lack of shrewdness makes you vulnerable to the craftiness of evildoers and leaves you ineffective as a servant of God. Remember, the devil seeks to destroy us. An appropriate and righteous shrewdness protects you from this—and equips you to protect the weak and innocent as well.

It's God's shrewdness that saves us in the end as it protects, preserves, and shields us from the devil's many schemes. Still, we play a role here. We must learn an appropriate level of shrewdness, so that our safety in God is twofold: we put our trust in Him daily, and we learn to be wise to the devil's schemes.

The Ultimate Shrewd Act

Putting Jesus on the cross to die for our sins was not only a great act of love from our God, but the shrewdest act in history—remarkably cunning and brilliant to the point that even the devil didn't see it coming. Satan was fooled into thinking he had won and was successful in destroying the only Savior for mankind, but the truth was exactly the opposite. Jesus's death on the cross made the saving possible, much to the shock and disappointment of the realm of evil. Had God not been the shrewd and brilliant God he is, we wouldn't be here today.

Because of this, those who put their trust in Jesus will become remarkable beings—"new creatures," as Scripture calls it. We'll be astonished at what he does with our hearts and minds, and all that he makes us out to be. And this will happen in part because God simply outsmarted the devil and his evil schemes.

What a brilliant, clever, and shrewd way in which He loves us.

Reflection Questions

In what ways does this chapter challenge your image of God, and what it means to be shrewd?

What are some examples in your life today where you can carry out appropriate levels of shrewdness, but still be good and kind to others?

Think of a situation where you trusted someone and were taken advantage of. How might you have benefited from being a bit shrewder?

Chapter 14

WHAT GRACE MAKES POSSIBLE

My favorite track and field events are pole vaulting and the high jump. I wasn't good at either but enjoy watching those who are.

In pole vaulting, the contestant holds a long flexible pole while running toward a designated launching point. Once he arrives, he places the base of the pole in a metal box in the ground, then uses the flexibility of that pole to catapult him or herself up and over the crossbar set high overhead. The goal is to clear the crossbar without knocking it off its supports. This crossbar can be set around seventeen feet high in collegiate competition. The world record as I write this is twenty feet, 2.5 inches.

The high jump is similar, except no pole is involved. The horizontal bar may be set at four feet or more above the ground. But in this case, the contestant can only leap from the natural spring of their own legs to clear the bar before them. It's harder than it sounds.

As each competitor clears the crossbar successfully in either event, the bar is then raised a notch as the next round of competition ensues. The crossbar continues to be raised until one of the competitors touches the bar in the slightest and fails to clear it outright. The one who clears the bar at its highest point is the winner of the event.

The process of raising the bar is obviously designed to bring out the highest level of achievement possible in each athlete. And in the process, each competitor is challenged and stretched beyond where they might be willing to go on their own. God's desire is to do the same with us, if we'll let Him.

Setting the Bar

Let's be honest: most of us don't like the bar being raised when it comes to the challenges in life—or facing any kind of bar in the first place. Life is hard enough, much more so if we're trying to rise higher through life's struggles. But that is God's call on our lives.

Some don't want to bother with excellence, however, and the hard work it takes to achieve it. There are times I certainly don't; it's part of being human. Those who achieve great things in this life, however, not only accept it, but understand that there is no other path to truly valuable living. Therefore, they embrace it.

Our culture in general is requiring less and less of people and running contrary to the call of excellence. The crossbar of life is slowly being lowered regarding what's considered acceptable language, holding criminal behavior accountable, as well as what's tolerated in the name of politics. How we manage personal integrity and conduct our affairs both publicly and privately is just not under the scrutiny it used to be. All of this can be viewed through the lens of lowering the bar of expectations within our society, and toward one another.

But when God's call is on your life, that call will move you in a direction contrary to the compromise of the world, and to rise to the highest levels of truth and integrity.

Raising the Bar

One of the most beautiful realizations upon surrendering to the love of God found in Jesus is knowing you're fully accepted, flaws and all. It is difficult to put into words, but there is this remarkable moment where one realizes that all past mistakes and sins are now washed away. Mere human utterances seem inadequate to express the peace that envelops the soul of the one who experiences such a miraculous liberation.

In this wonderful forgiveness from our loving God, however, we also understand that His intention is to go to work and create a new person altogether. And this process is meant to eventually bring you and me to a state of excellence, even perfection.

This is where Christians can get disillusioned, even misled. Some think that because of grace, there is no need to change, overcome, or strive for excellence. God's will, however, is not just to save us from our sins, but to transform us into new beings of a higher state—a holy state.

We can't make this happen on our own, of course; it's the work of God in us. But we're to do our part and strive for it appropriately as we yield to the miraculous process of redemption.

The Process of Redemption

As with our track and field events, God slowly raises the bar over time with the believer. He expects us to improve our skills of living and walking as Christians over time, and to overcome all obstacles that keep us from His best.

Some Christians struggle to accept this part of God's grace. And because they don't strive to give God their very best, or allow Him to work in them, their lives are disappointing and fruitless. But as we embrace the call to excellence and work to overcome, a real purpose fills our lives and much fruit abounds within. And that's when life gets really good.

> What shall we say, then? Shall we go on sinning so that grace may increase? By no means! We are those who have died to sin; how can we live in it any longer? (Romans 6:1–2)

We are *not* called to magnify the need for grace. Rather, we are to live in a way that shows what grace makes possible. As Jesus tells us, "Be perfect, therefore, as your heavenly Father is perfect" (Matthew 5:48).

We are to strive for excellence not because we need to earn anything, but because we've been given a spirit of perfection in Christ Jesus. We need to learn to live from that holy and flawless spirit: "For everyone to whom much is given, from him much will be required" (Luke 12:48, NKJV).

Compassion with High Expectations

I have noticed two crucial elements in God's amazing love: compassion, and the process of calling us higher. I mention these two for a reason.

Our gentle God always shows compassion, but He never coddles. Take that in for a second. God knows the difference between real empathy, and over-pampering someone. Humanly, we get those mixed up. We often think one is the other.

Compassion is a reminder that God truly empathizes and knows what our pain feels like. He will always take our hopes, desires, and fears into consideration along with any demands He lays upon us. Remember, He walked in the flesh while on Earth, and experienced every temptation we do.

Coddling, however, is different. It requires nothing of people. It impedes character development, and stifles maturity and growth. And it shows respect for the person only, not the truth or what's best for someone—which, ultimately, is remarkably unloving.

I'll be frank: God has allowed me to go through some excruciating things in my past, even as a child. And there were times when I questioned whether He really loved me because of those things. But as I've hung in there with God and begun to see the fruit that comes from trusting Him, I can now see the fruit that's come from those tough experiences. This has allowed me to see that God was there all along, even in the suffering and unfair times. He gave me what I needed to endure. But he didn't coddle. And I thank Him for that . . . *now*.

There's a lot I wish I had been spared from. But if I had been, I would not have matured and overcome the way I have, and really needed to, which is paramount to who I am today. God can be tough, I won't lie, but it's love all the same.

God wastes nothing, including any moments of suffering we may endure. He utilizes every bit of it for our good. And because of God's love shown through his willingness to forgive every sin, He raises the bar and gives us the tools to rise to that bar of excellence.

God's Way

In our society, we have it exactly backward. We sometimes lack real compassion for the plight of those who suffer, while simultaneously over-pampering them and requiring nothing of them. But God is not like us. His love is perfect, whole, and complete, without bias or confusion. It's a love that bears real fruit. He simply loves from a holy place within Himself. Because of this, we can trust His love.

He cares deeply for each of us, empathizes with our struggles, and yet also nudges us toward right living and better character. He compels us to live with integrity and selflessness, and shows us how to treat others. He sets our sights on perfection—and expects us to seek it too.

God knows when to encourage, and when to rebuke, when to show compassion and when to lay down the law. He's always calling us to a higher way of living, and to a better way of loving those around us. God raises the bar so that the best may be brought out in each of us. Only then can we be true witnesses to His power and love. Don't resist this call—embrace it. The love of God expressed through His grace has made this possible. Don't waste it.

Yes, we're called by God to seek the perfect spirit that resides within Him, and now in us. That's what the Holy Spirit is, the very spirit who emanates from our holy God. We do this with humility, knowing that we can't do it in our own strength, but only with the spirit and help of our perfect and powerful God.

Grace didn't save us; our loving God did through the blood of Christ Jesus. But by His power expressed through His love and grace, we are able to seek the perfection of God, and be our best for Him and others. If you don't feel you have God's Spirit, Jesus says this:

> If you then, though you are evil, know how to give good gifts to your children, how much more will your Father in heaven give the *Holy Spirit* to those who ask him! (Luke 11:13, emphasis added)

In God's love, He asks us to do what we can't do without Him, and that is to become perfect. It is a test of faith to turn away from our human limitations and set our gaze upon the heart and mind of our perfect God. But it is here that we find the very best of who we are in Christ Jesus, and who Jesus is in us. And in the process, we discover all that is possible for those who ask for and receive the Holy Spirit. Our God wants nothing less. And His grace makes it possible.

What a remarkable way He loves those who trust in Him.

Reflection Questions

How do you feel about God forgiving our sins through grace, but also calling us to the perfection found in Christ Jesus? How do you reconcile the two?

When do you feel tempted to lower the bar of integrity in your life—and do you use God's grace as an excuse to do so?

As you move forward in your life, in what areas do you feel called to raise the bar and strive to give God your very best, and with the help of His Spirit?

Chapter 15

THE ULTIMATE HERESY

*H*eresy is described as any teaching or idea that deviates from foundational Christianity, especially as described in Scripture. It would include the promotion of new doctrine or a religious concept that is contrary to God's Word, the Holy Bible. This can occur in a variety of ways, and to different degrees of severity.

There is one heresy, however, that is most egregious of them all—and that is to place God in any other light than love.

The Pharisee Problem

The ultimate heresy is best illustrated in the way the Jews of Jesus's day represented God to the masses and carried out religious oppression in the name of God. Jesus's own interactions with them reveal how God Himself felt about the falsehoods they embodied. There was no group Jesus was harder on, and He reserved the most severe condemnation for these religious zealots:

> "Brood of vipers! How can you, being evil, speak good things? For out of the abundance of the heart the mouth speaks" (Matthew 12:24, NKJV).

What's interesting about these words from Jesus is that the Pharisees were the most obedient people on Earth—in a sense. They were certainly the most disciplined in both their personal and religious life. Their adherence to the law and to Jewish customs was impeccable and would make our religious behavior today look sloppy by comparison. They tithed without hesitation, as much as 30 percent some years. They fasted not once but twice a week. They were meticulous in their attention to not only the Law of Moses but to the hundreds of additional rules and regulations they had added over time. I'm not sure anyone has been more religious than the Jews of Jesus's day. And they compromised this for no one, not even the Romans who ruled over them. From a religious standpoint, they were admired for their remarkable adherence to their laws and customs.

Jesus found one major thing missing, however, and it happened to be the biggest thing of all: love. More specifically, a genuine love for people in general. In one exchange, Jesus made the point this way:

> And behold, there was a man who had a withered hand. And [the Pharisees] asked Him, saying, "Is it lawful to heal on the Sabbath?"—that they might accuse Him.
>
> Then He said to them, "What man is there among you who has one sheep, and if it falls into a pit on the Sabbath, will not lay hold of it and lift it out? Of how much more value then is a man than a sheep? Therefore it is lawful to do good on the Sabbath." Then He said to the man, "Stretch out your hand." And he stretched it out, and it was restored as whole as the other. (Matthew 12:10–13, NKJV)

How important was love to Jesus? And how much of His ministry was really about the people He interacted with?

Jesus resisted the call to bring down millions of angels to fight on His behalf. He refused the prompting to establish a human army that He may resist and overtake Rome. He didn't demand money from his followers. He didn't give speeches designed to raise millions for the latest building project. He refused any kind of religious authority, position, or title. He refused fame, glory, and wealth, all of which He could have easily attained and rightfully so. He also refused to exercise revenge against anyone who had harmed Him.

The one thing Jesus did consistently insist on was to demonstrate love to the oppressed and hurting around Him. He even prayed that God would forgive those who had put Him on the cross to face a horrible death. These are not the actions of a religious man, but of a loving God. This may be one of the clearest pictures of the heart of God, and the way He loves. And Jesus is that exact representation of the Father: "He who has seen Me has seen the Father" (John 14:9, NKJV).

A Message in the Word

For our God, it's always been about love, and this is displayed even in how the Bible itself is laid out. From Genesis, the first book in the Bible, to the last book of Revelation, God tells a story of His generous gift of life, and His desire to redeem a lost people back to Himself—all for the sake of His love for His creation.

For thousands of years, as told through the Old Testament, God spoke mostly through a few patriarchs and prophets along the way. In the New Testament, we learn through the Gospels of Matthew, Mark, Luke, and John of the love of Jesus, His only Son.

From the written record of those who walked with Jesus or lived during His time, we are given letters that have now become canonized Scripture. And these remarkable vestiges of Christian history tell us much about God's love.

Even the book of Revelation, the final book in the Bible, calls the various churches within the region to return to their "first love," meaning the love a believer receives when first called, because it's so easy to make it about other things. Yes, love is central to the Christian experience, and it is central from the very beginning of God's call on our life.

As this God-inspired literary achievement called the Bible crescendos at the epistles of John, toward the end of the Bible, we learn that all things hinge on God's persistent love for us, and our love for Him. More than any other book in the Bible, 1 John reveals that the wheel of life is not complete until love flows in both directions—from God to us, and from us back to God. All we learn and know about God can be summed up in three words: "God is love" (1 John 4:8).

Reflection Questions

What harm might be done if God is presented in a light other than love?

What are some of your first thoughts when considering that God is love at His very core?

How aware were you that the story of God is primarily a story of God's great love for His children? How did this chapter change your perspective?

How have you misunderstood God's love in the past? What impact has that had on your life?

Chapter 16

A WILLINGNESS TO SUFFER

hen I think of the various levels at which we all suffer, I believe both God's Word and life itself reveals three main levels. One would be a suffering caused by our own human nature and the poor choices we make. The second level would be the poor choices or actions of others and the effects those choices have on us personally.

The third level of suffering, however, is chosen by an individual for the purpose of delivering a benefit for another and ultimately for their good. This is sacrificial love. Though suffering is common and all around us, an intentional love-based suffering may be rarer.

Suffering happens to all of us, of course, and in different ways, regardless of socioeconomic status or where one lives on the planet. We spend much of our lives trying to avoid any kind of suffering or discomfort. Not many will choose to leave a place of comfort and embrace suffering intentionally for their own gain, let alone for the gain of someone else.

There is one, however, who not only endures suffering but who willingly entered into suffering on the behalf of others. And that is our Creator God. And the reason for doing so is no less than astonishing.

God Suffers

In the second and third chapters of the book of Genesis, we read the account of Adam and Eve and their disobedience to God in the garden of Eden. Once they were placed in the garden, God told them they were free to eat fruit from any tree in the garden, except the tree of knowledge of good and evil. If they did, God warned, they would surely die.

The serpent Satan then shows up and says to the woman, "You will not surely die. For God knows when you eat from it your eyes will be opened, and you will be like God, knowing good and evil" (Genesis 3:4–5, NKJV). Eve decides to believe the serpent over God, eats fruit from the forbidden tree, and gives some to Adam to eat as well. Just as God said, their eyes were suddenly opened to both good and evil—and thus to a darkness they had previously not known.

As shame and self-awareness set in, the pure and holy state of mind God had originally given them had been soiled and now forgotten. For their own protection, and perhaps to keep Eden holy, God removed them from the garden. They were now to live the remainder of their lives in a cursed and barren land. They had entered the realm of mortality and were doomed to eventually face death. Suffering amongst humanity had now begun.

As I read this account in God's Word, I noticed that God's response to Adam and Eve's disobedience seemed void of emotion. Absent of anger. And missing any sign of sorrow or regret—not to mention surprise. It's as if God had prepared for such an outcome, if not entirely expected it.

Fast-forward to chapter six of Genesis. Many years had passed since the garden event, and the earth was now populated with many people, some say millions. Noah is now the central character in this time when "the LORD saw how great the wickedness of the human race had become on the earth, and that every inclination of the thoughts of the human heart was only evil all the time" (Genesis 6:5).

Upon this time in history, we first begin to sense disappointment within the Creator's own heart, even pain: "The LORD regretted that he had made human beings on the earth, and his heart was deeply troubled . . . 'for I regret that I have made them.'" (Genesis 6:6–7).

A Relatable God

My view of God changed dramatically the day I first read the words of God's own troubled heart and subsequent regret for making mankind. After all, they were God's children made in His likeness. For me, this changed everything. For God was no longer a distant, judging, and unfeeling God abiding in some cosmic bubble of pleasure somewhere. He was now a God capable of pain, who had joined us in the realm of suffering. He clearly cared about the choices we made, and the outcomes they brought. This made Him real to me, and relatable.

God apparently feels pain when we embrace sinful behavior and suffers for our poor choices. I began to ask myself, what father wouldn't suffer as he watched his children make choices that only brought failure, struggle, and disillusionment? Choices that are contrary to life, love, freedom, peace, and joy? I now understood that God has his own heart on the line for His creation, and for that reason was willing to suffer on our behalf.

I believe we make huge leaps toward wisdom when we accept that suffering is not experienced merely on the human plane, but on the "God plane" as well.

And His suffering continued through to His son Jesus. In fact, the suffering of God, as experienced through Jesus, had been prophesied hundreds of years before He had appeared on Earth: "He was despised and rejected by mankind, a man of suffering, and familiar with pain. Like one from whom people hide their faces he was despised, and we held him in low esteem. Surely he took up our pain and bore our suffering" (Isaiah 53:3–4).

A Life of Purpose

Have you ever been a part of something that was very difficult, and yet for a good cause? Maybe you helped someone through a tough time, built something that required sweat and struggle, or endured a difficult trial on behalf of someone you cared about. It might have even been extremely uncomfortable for you. Even so, you wouldn't trade the experience for anything because it was laced with real meaning and value. The cause and purpose outweighed the discomfort or difficulty. Plus, we may have even matured through that difficulty. This is a type of redemptive suffering.

Some deal with the challenges of parenting, staying in a struggling marriage, helping a friend through a trial of some kind, or helping someone step away from an addiction. There can be real pain and even suffering through these experiences, but they're worth it. The people we care about are worth it.

I remember the excruciating experience of visiting a family member in the hospital after a major car accident. I came very close to passing out upon seeing her because the injuries were so severe. She was barely recognizable as she lay in the hospital bed unconscious, struggling to survive. But she needed to know she wasn't going to suffer alone. It was hard to endure, but I never regretted it. When love is the driver, however difficult, it is filled with a purpose and power that exceeds the discomfort that often comes with it.

I see the same when natural disasters or acts of terrorism land upon our shores. Horrible things happen, suffering ensues, but people spring forth with love and purpose that our society rarely witnesses. The pain and loss are real, but the real purpose for life and love rises in the hearts of those bent on serving, even when it's hurtful.

This, I believe, is one of God's recipes for a pleasure-filled life. Honorable suffering and authentic purpose go hand in hand. And our loving Creator is right there in the middle of it with us.

Intolerable Suffering

I've discovered that it's not suffering in itself that seems unbearable; it's the thought that we're suffering alone, or without meaning. It is better to know suffering that has a purpose than to live out a selfish life that is of little benefit to others.

Because of God's willingness to suffer alongside me, I now know I'm not alone. There's a reason for every tear, every hurt, and every experience that brings pain and discomfort, and God is faithful to bring about good from all of it.

I also know that true love happens because a loving God deems you and me worthy of His own suffering. He endures a great deal on our behalf, perhaps to a degree we'll never fully grasp. But it's best evidenced by His willingness to walk in true love-based suffering for the children He loves.

Without His love-based suffering, you and I would not be redeemed. It's just another way He shows his remarkable love.

Reflection Questions

What do you feel when considering God's willingness to suffer on your behalf?

What do you think of a God who loves and sacrifices in such a way?

How does this change your outlook on your own suffering, or add meaning to any suffering you've experienced personally?

Chapter 17

A HEART RECEPTIVE TO GOD'S LOVE

*Woe to you Pharisees, because you give God a tenth of
your mint, rue and all other kinds of garden herbs, but
you neglect justice and the love of God.*

—Luke 11:42

During the early days of my Christian calling, I saw my walk with God primarily through a legalistic lens. The focus was on keeping God's laws as close to the letter as possible. Looking back decades later, however, God had a higher goal for me than just being a good religious man. It turns out that He's far more concerned with whether I'm willing to be receptive to His will, and especially to His love.

If perfection were God's initial aim, He could have made you and I perfect from the beginning. He's God; He knows how to create perfection via a simple command. In fact, He made the angels perfect. And before the devil became who he is today, he was a beautiful and powerful angel. Even Adam and Eve were initially without sin while in the garden of Eden, right before they made a decision that would change the world for millennia to come.

All of them, however, betrayed God in one form or another. The great and perfect angel who would become the devil was found to be the biggest traitor of all time. He tried to overthrow God Himself and take His throne. Even though they were made perfect, one-third of the angels abandoned God and joined forces with the devil. And Adam and Eve chose to trust the devil over God. They all were initially perfect, but ultimately were found to be disloyal.

So you see, God can create anything and anyone that He wants, and instantly if preferred. He can adorn them with many godly traits, and even make them in His image. But when it comes to creating beings who are driven by love for God and others, well, that's a different matter, and a more complicated one. And it turns out to be the most important one of all.

As our God desires that we know that He loves us, He needs to know whether we'll be loyal enough to not only walk with Him, but return that love back to Him and others. Why does the concern of loyalty center around love? Love, as it turns out, is the best measure of loyalty, of what we'll fully give our hearts over to. Take a look at what God's Word says regarding both love and an important component to loyalty, obedience:

> And this is love: that we walk in obedience to his commands. As you have heard from the beginning, his command is that you walk in love. (2 John 6)

A Risky Gift

Can you see how both love and obedience are inherently linked, and how they both reveal our loyalty to God? We don't hear this enough, but who and what we love reveals our true allegiance more than any other attribute of God's nature.

In order to test the waters of love and faithfulness, however, God must give us a certain amount of power. And that incredible power is called free will. This gift allows us to choose to love God on our own accord, or not. The only way to find out where our loyalties lie is to give us the freedom to deny Him, and that's where things get messy. Loyalty cannot be created or arranged for, only chosen from a place of complete freedom.

You may not like the world we live in, or the mess that people make of it. Only within this landscape, however, does God discover where our loyalties lie, and if our love is genuine.

Some believe that God already knows who will remain faithful to Him; others believe that God doesn't know until we choose. Either way, the truth of what we stand for is established during this life, and we reap the rewards of that decision, whether in the negative or positive. After all, life in this contradictory environment called the world has a way of causing us to eventually get on the side of either good or evil. Whatever our choice, we're responsible for the outcome.

As you may have noticed, God takes a different approach with us than He did with the angels and even Adam and Eve. We are weak and sinful from the beginning, and true perfection and righteousness will not be given up front. Rather, it will happen only if we choose it over evil during our lives. When we do, God is greatly pleased because we chose Him while in the throes of a dark and an alluring world.

The Priority of Love

As we choose God and His love over evil, we quickly discover that He desires to shepherd us, protect us, and take care of us, all from the place of His great love. There's so much more to it than just fixing us, or even making us perfect. Notice what Jesus said concerning the Father's heart for His people:

> Jerusalem, Jerusalem, you who kill the prophets and stone those sent to you, how often I have longed to gather your children together, as a hen gathers her chicks under her wings, and you were not willing. (Matthew 23:37)

This obviously does not come from the heart of a legalistic God, but from a compassionate, affectionate, and a wonderfully loving God toward those who will gather themselves under His protective wings.

Here's the beautiful thing: the more I learn to trust in this remarkable love, the more the perfecting process carries on as a natural side effect of abiding in Him. If I resist God's love, if my trust for Him wanes, or I obsess over being perfect, the redemption process slows or stalls altogether. I couldn't wrap my mind around this at first, but in time it's become clearer. All along, God was steering me toward trusting in His love for me, away from a mere technical or legalistic form of perfection. But my heart was hard; I couldn't see His love for me. Thankfully, He's softened my heart over time, which has allowed me to better know and experience His love.

So if you're not there yet, give it time. Ask God to help you to feel and to know His faithful love. He'll answer that prayer.

Sadly, not everyone wants the gospel to be a story of love and loyalty. It might not seem practical or doctrinally meaty enough for those who prefer a more "religious" experience. But if one tries to religionize the heart and plan of God, they'll be disappointed.

In reality, love is at the heart of the gospel, who and what God is, and what matters to God the most.

> And now these three remain: faith, hope and love. But the greatest of these is love. (1 Corinthians 13:13)

As I continue to experience new levels of God's love and faithfulness after more than forty years with Him, an internal healing continues as well. New levels of joy and purpose are always just around the bend. With each passing year, I'm seeing new levels of freedom which I couldn't have imagined before. The goodness of God simply never stops, and never fails to reach new heights within.

The more I abide in His love, the better my health gets. I've struggled with many ailments since birth, but over time my health has improved a lot. I have to do my part and change some habits; my body is not perfect, but it has vastly improved the closer I've gotten to God. It's an incredible experience, and it always brings me back to God's love for me.

If we fixate on our own flaws and are anxious to correct them, especially apart from God's timing, we'll fail in our efforts. But when we learn to bask in His faithful love and trust in His provision for us daily, a healing of the heart and mind will happen over time. But we must do our part and keep abiding in Him. Nothing could be more amazing, more fulfilling, or more important. Remember, we're the patient; He's the doctor.

God doesn't just want us to be right, but to be right in His love. This will only happen as we remain receptive to His love and are willing to abide in it. He needs us to understand primarily that this is about His love for us, and about our learning to love Him in return. Only then are we able to bring that love to others, and with the right perspective.

God's Real Agenda

The priority of God's heart is concisely revealed in the one commandment that Jesus says fulfills the law of God:

> Love the Lord your God with all your heart and with all your soul and with all your mind. This is the first and greatest commandment. (Matthew 22:37–38)

We can be religious, generous, have faith, be moral, and yet still resist His love and fail to love others. If we do, we've failed to understand the message that God has not only for us but the world.

The apostle Paul, a former legalist and major contributor to the New Testament, came to this remarkable revelation himself:

> If I speak in the tongues of men or of angels, but do not have love, I am only a resounding gong or a clanging cymbal. If I have the gift of prophecy and can fathom all mysteries and all knowledge, and if I have a faith that can move mountains, but do not have love, I am nothing. If I give all I possess to the poor and give over my body to hardship that I may boast, but do not have love, I gain nothing. (1 Corinthians 13:1–3)

God's Definition of Perfection

If love were not first established in our hearts, we would become "perfect" in a religious or legalistic sense, which creates its own kind of monster. Remember the proud Pharisees we talked about earlier, and how they loved their laws, money, and animals more than other people? That's what we would become. Because love had not first been established in their hearts, they ironically became the furthest thing from God, and a gross misrepresentation of the Father's heart. As a result, they despised the very one sent to save them: Jesus. They didn't recognize Jesus as coming from God's kingdom, as the perfect representation of God the Father.

Whether in religious arrogance or immoral decadence, pride remains. The first group basks in self-righteousness; the second thinks they have a right to exercise their free will however they want. True Christian love, however, must always be expressed within the guidelines given in God's Word. And showing love is never an excuse to compromise those Christian ideals. The moment we do, it is no longer godly love.

Real Power for Those Who Receive God's Love

When we're receptive to God's love and we allow it to work in our lives, we'll see real change. Broken relationships can mend, selfishness can dissipate, and fear can be conquered, all as a result of God's powerful and life-changing love.

I have gone to God in the middle of the night countless times with various fears, tears, and requests, and He has never failed to comfort, encourage, and answer everything I've ever brought to Him, sometimes with miraculous results. His love for us is faithful, consistent, and powerful. I hope you'll seek His loving heart today, and begin to know His love the way I have come to know it.

Godly love heals our minds, balances our emotions, and soothes our wounds. Love delivers us from self, lifts us from the pit of despair, and untangles us from the trappings of life. All we have to do is take every hurt to Him in prayer, and then obey what He asks.

Love sharpens our gaze, reminds us who we are, and liberates us from a life of confusion. It will deliver us from the darkness that threatens to destroy. Even if you're in evil's powerful grip, call upon His holy name and He will rescue you.

God's love gives us right perspective and takes away the delusions of a false outlook. Turn to the God of love and your point of view will become brighter.

Godly love will make you a better parent, a truer friend, and a better human being. God's love will make you care how you come across to others and deliver you from the delusion of serving self alone. Love sets all things right in our lives and in our hearts, and will help us steer clear of evil temptation—but only when we seek and abide in His love. Choose to be a seeker of God and His faithful love. When you do, you'll discover another incredible way He loves.

Reflection Questions

What connections do you see between love and loyalty?

As you examine your own heart, do you find it open to receiving God's love and interacting with God on that level? Explain.

In what ways do you feel you've sought out the love of God?

What steps can you take to be more receptive to God's love and movement in your own heart?

Chapter 18

THE GAIN IN LOSING THE WORLD

Better is a dinner of herbs where love is, than a fatted calf with hatred.

—Proverbs 15:17, NKJV

There are a variety of changes to our world that have occurred over time as a result of Jesus's influence. For one, He demonstrated that men, women, and children are equally valued by God and equally loved, and that society should reflect that equality—which was quite a leap for mankind during the time Jesus walked the earth.

Jesus also taught that a religious temple or building is not the dwelling place of God. Rather, it is in the actual hearts and minds of those who believe in Christ Jesus as their savior.

There's another significant change Jesus brought to the world, and few things affect our lives more: the idea of what constitutes true and lasting wealth.

Wealth's Shadowy Nature

We all need some level of physical wealth in order to survive; here we can almost all agree. We all need food, water, clothing, transportation, housing, etc. Wealth is not just a desire; it's an inherent need. However, how much wealth someone has or needs is a different matter.

Some believe the amount of wealth someone has is of the greatest concern. I've learned, however, to concern myself less with how much someone has, and more on how much prominence one gives physical or monetary wealth. Whether one is rich, poor, or somewhere in between, wealth can hold an unhealthy sense of prominence in one's heart. And there lies the most important issue when it comes to wealth.

Physical wealth never lasts. Money, for instance, tends to dry up more quickly than we expect. One minute there's plenty to pay the bills; the next minute we're wondering how we'll make it through the next thirty days. Physical wealth in any form can disappear like a vapor in the wind. We must understand that this is by design.

The fleeting nature of physical or monetary wealth is part of what God wants us to see and experience. As important as it is, God wants us to focus on a far superior form of wealth—a type of wealth that lasts and never disappears. To understand this better, we must first look at the idea of wealth in general, and what it represents.

The Idea of Wealth

Beyond food, water, clothing, and shelter, wealth is really just an idea. Paper money, gold, silver, stocks, and bonds are only of interest to us because they represent an image we have of being wealthy, of having more than we need—and perhaps, of having more control of our lives. These things have very little inherent value in themselves, however, if any. Even land is not useful until we plant crops on it or build a house. Really, it's just dirt until we put it to use.

When I watch the "buy gold" commercials on TV, and hear them describe how they'll deliver your gold to your front door, I laugh inside and ask myself, "What would I do with a bar of gold in my house?" I mean, really? But they offer it as if we can't wait to have real gold in our home. Make no mistake, they're trying to leverage a transitory idea of wealth that some fall for.

I realize that buying gold is viewed by some as a place to park your money as a hedge against inflation. For many, however—and maybe all of us on one level or another—it's the perception of being or feeling wealthy that we're after, and the fleeting sense of security we think wealth will provide.

Whatever our perception of wealth is, we're all looking for something much deeper than monetary or physical wealth. Something more personally fulfilling, and certainly something beyond just meeting our physical needs. In a way, monetary wealth analogizes what we really want, but it's not the thing itself. Monetary wealth was never meant to provide spiritual fulfillment, but some seek it as if it can. If we do this, we're merely trying to lay grip on a shadow, and missing the real thing in the process.

Jesus's Idea of Wealth

Jesus had a lot to say about wealth, the world's misunderstanding of what it is, and its real purpose. He also contrasted real wealth with symbolic material wealth. In the process, Jesus pointed us toward a different kind of wealth: "Everyone who drinks this water will be thirsty again, but whoever drinks the water I give them will never thirst" (John 4:13).

For thousands of years, gold, silver, and rubies were primary measures of one's wealth, along with animals and land. Even the wealth of God's people, the ancient Israelites of old, was often measured in these terms. But Jesus turned that entire concept on its head by bringing a truth the world had never heard of—at least not predominantly—and challenging His listeners to instead pursue this kind of wealth:

> [D]o not set your heart on what you will eat or drink; do not worry about it. For the pagan world runs after all such things, and your Father knows that you need them. But seek his kingdom, and these things will be given to you as well.
>
> Do not be afraid, little flock, for your Father has been pleased to give you the kingdom. Sell your possessions and give to the poor. Provide purses for yourselves that will not wear out, a treasure in heaven that will never fail, where no thief comes near and no moth destroys. (Luke 12:29–33)

Jesus was clearly calling people to think beyond just physical wealth, toward the greater need to seek God's kingdom—which is not only greater than physical wealth but the reality that monetary wealth actually points to. Jesus was aware of how easily we are deceived by the riches of this world, and our proclivity to see it as a false sense of security. He spoke to this fact directly:

> And [Jesus] told them this parable: "The ground of a certain rich man yielded an abundant harvest. He thought to himself, 'What shall I do? I have no place to store my crops.'

"Then he said, 'This is what I'll do. I will tear down my barns and build bigger ones, and there I will store my surplus grain. And I'll say to myself, "You have plenty of grain laid up for many years. Take life easy; eat, drink and be merry."'

"But God said to him, 'You fool! This very night your life will be demanded from you. Then who will get what you have prepared for yourself?'

"This is how it will be with whoever stores up things for themselves but is not rich toward God." (Luke 12:16–21)

Protecting Ourselves from the Lies of Material Wealth

I don't believe Jesus was slamming wealth or prosperity here. Rather, He was rebuking the concept of setting our hearts on the world's idea of wealth, and placing our personal sense of security on that wealth. If we obsess over thinking that some people have too much, we're missing Jesus's point. How we prioritize wealth in our hearts is His concern.

> Watch out! Be on guard against all kinds of greed; life does not consist in the abundance of possessions. (Luke 12:15)

I can recall the times I've put my hope in some business concept or opportunity I thought would bring me great wealth, and then suffered deep sadness when it didn't work out. I foolishly attached my joy and vitality, and perhaps some level of security, to whether some venture was successful or not. But in God's great love, He's trained that way of thinking out of me, and rescued me from the deadly trap of giving worldly wealth too much credit for the full life I want to live.

The problem was that I had mixed up monetary wealth with the value of life that I had already been given. This confusion can happen with any form of physical wealth, and with any amount. The problem isn't abundance as much as it is thinking that any form of physical wealth is ever going to be enough to fill our souls: "life is more than food, and the body more than clothes" (Luke 12:23). We cannot add to life itself; we can only receive it and live it out. As Jesus went on to say, "seek his kingdom, and these things will be given to you as well" (Luke 12:31).

Jesus has nothing against wealth. In fact, He states that He gladly gives it to us. But He wants us to enjoy physical wealth in its proper context, and with a right sense of priority. There is nothing wrong with prospering from an honest and acceptable endeavor, especially if it's pursued with integrity and excellence. I know many godly people who work and prosper in this way. And I don't think there should ever be a limit on how much one can make or prosper—that is between them and God, especially if they are not defrauding others by aiming for unreasonable profits.

But if our aim is solely to get rich, and failing to love our neighbor in the process, we're treading on dangerous ground. That approach will bear rotten fruit.

> Whoever loves money never has enough; whoever loves wealth is never satisfied with their income. (Ecclesiastes 5:10)

> [B]ut the worries of this life, the deceitfulness of wealth and the desires for other things come in and choke the word, making it unfruitful. (Mark 4:19)

A friend of mine told me years ago that he wanted to know how to become a wealthy and successful man. He sought out a family friend who had achieved great wealth and success and asked him for an interview. After the interview, my friend told me that he was surprised by what his friend had told him. The wealthy friend expressed that he would do anything to be free of his great wealth and all the obligations and expectations that came with it. Because of his position as a wealthy and influential businessman, many depended on him, to the point that it became a burden. Those ties, obligations, and expectations of others controlled his life and robbed him of his freedom. There were many people who had been instrumental in him becoming a success and attaining great wealth, and they "owned him" as a result. He couldn't just walk away, he explained; too much was at stake. If he did, it would adversely affect too many people. Because of this, he felt trapped.

My friend did walk away from that interview, however—and with a very different perspective on wealth and the price one might pay for attaining it. In fact, he began to think less about worldly wealth and more about another kind of wealth: the one Jesus spoke of. And that is the wealth of freedom. Our conversations from that point on were more about those kinds of gifts, and how physical wealth can actually rob us in this regard. We must understand that the temptation of wealth is a trap, and meant to get you off the path of life.

> For what profit is it to a man if he gains the whole world, and loses his own soul? Or what will a man give in exchange for his soul? (Matthew 16:26, NKJV)

Coming Out of the World

One of the biggest themes in God's Word is the challenge to come out of the world and its many trappings. And that is a challenge to not only avoid the deception of monetary wealth, but to think and live differently in regard to God's idea of wealth. That's easier said than done. The world is not just a place we reside in but something that resides in us, in our very nature. Therefore, a significant aspect of the redemption process is the removal of the world from our beings, including the false and dangerous paradigm of worldly riches.

But in God's great love, He knows how to deliver us from such a trap. We must put our trust in Him that He may do so. And, we must know His Word and do what it says.

One of the main problems with monetary wealth is that it has a way of taking our eye off the spiritual ball. I have known many people in my life whose main focus was on money, and others whose main focus was on the will of God. I've never met anyone who can do both. Jesus made this statement: "No one can serve two masters. Either you will hate the one and love the other, or you will be devoted to the one and despise the other. You cannot serve both God and money" (Matthew 6:24). Sadly, many have fallen away from the faith because physical wealth won out. But I don't believe that will happen to you. Take a stand and make a choice. Choose God over worldly wealth.

God's Idea of Wealth

This all begs the question: What kind of wealth does God want us to focus on, exactly? In His great love, Jesus came to this world in part to show us what real wealth looks like, and how it's directly connected to His kingdom, not this world. To understand what Jesus wants to do in our hearts and minds, we must first understand a simple truth that is contrary to the world's idea of wealth.

The authentic life Jesus offers is lived out from within our beings, not from something outside ourselves. True life is lived from the inside out, not from the outside in. Monetary wealth is the opposite: it comes to us from the outside. Because of this, it cannot satisfy or fill us in any meaningful way. It has its value—we need monetary wealth in order to function in this world—but it cannot well up from within our beings and give us what we all desperately need from God. It is not what we were made for. Our loving God offers us the kind of wealth that springs up from within—a kind of wealth only He can provide: "whoever drinks the water I give them will never thirst. Indeed, the water I give them will become in them a spring of water welling up to eternal life" (John 4:14). Here are just a few examples of what that kind of wealth brings into our lives:

- salvation from our sins
- preparation for authentic wealth today, and in God's coming kingdom
- peace resulting from the full acceptance and love of God
- authentic joy, regardless of finances or circumstances
- the comfort and joy of family
- friendships with faithful and honest people
- physical well-being and health
- a life that matures over time, and overcomes sin and flaws
- plentiful resources to provide for family, God's work, and others in need
- great favor from God in all aspects of life

- protection from the deceptions and lies of this world
- being filled with His wisdom in all matters of life
- freedom from darkness, evil strongholds, and worldly philosophies that deceive

The Streets of God

If you want to know what God thinks of a valuable substance like gold, look at what He does with it in His future kingdom, as stated in Revelation 21:21: He paves the streets with it. I love that. We'll be walking on it. Not trading it, not buying and selling it, not hoarding it, and certainly not giving our lives over to the pursuit of it. As beautiful as gold is, it's just pavement to God. In His kingdom, God demoted gold to its proper place as a beautiful but practical substance. In God's great kingdom, and in His great love for us, He's literally placing gold under our feet.

But it's also interesting to note that even in God's perfect and holy kingdom, He doesn't abandon physical wealth. In fact, He increases it. But He does put it in its proper context. You won't have to pay a fortune for it or have it delivered to your house. No, you'll be surrounded by it. You'll be walking on it. It will belong to everyone.

There's important messaging here about what God thinks of us exalting gold to the status this world gives it, and making it so that only the megarich can have access to it. And perhaps one can draw even more analogies than what I've pointed out here. But at the very most, gold is only a symbol of beauty, prosperity, and lasting wealth, nothing more. And that goes for every kind of physical or monetary wealth. God Himself is the real prize and essence of life. All that He contains within Himself, and offers to us, is of far greater value and is the real wealth we long for, and should be pursuing.

Putting on the Robe of Godly Wealth

God desires to clothe us with life, truth, faith, hope, and love, which are the authentic and lasting elements of true wealth. I have known so many wealthy people in my life, and the family I was raised in was one of them. We didn't take a private jet on vacation or sip lattes everywhere we went, but we did pretty well. But I have known very few wealthy people who were genuinely happy and alive, and very few who were clothed with what our loving God wants to give to those who seek Him.

> I counsel you to buy from me gold refined in the fire, so you can become rich; and white clothes to wear, so you can cover your shameful nakedness. (Revelation 3:18)

This scripture gives us a glimpse into how God desires to "clothe" you and me. It involves so much more than an Armani suit or a Gucci purse. No, it's holiness. Washing us of our sins. Binding up our wounded hearts and minds. In His great love, He will cleanse and purify His children, and prepare us to enter His holy kingdom.

Our Reality in Jesus

How does our faith and trust in Jesus keep us from the deceptive nature of worldly wealth? Because when our hearts and minds are set on Him and His holy Word, they are set on the reality of all things. And Jesus *is* that reality. This in part is what it means when Jesus the Christ is called our Savior. Without Jesus's influence in our lives, we simply won't have the wherewithal to combat, outsmart or outflank the enemy and the deceptions of this world. And they are many. "These are a shadow of the things that were to come; the reality, however, is found in Christ" (Colossians 2:17).

In God's great love, He's offered His son to us that we may not be deceived by the trap of focusing alone on monetary wealth, and to know instead the true elements of authentic and lasting wealth. When we abide in Christ and are protected from the lies of the world's view of wealth, we experience a freedom, peace, hope and love that's far beyond what all the gold in the world could ever bring. And that is true wealth, God's way.

Reflection Questions

In what ways does this chapter challenge your view of material wealth, as opposed to spiritual wealth with God?

Do you feel your pursuit or interaction with wealth is balanced? Explain.

In what ways has your particular level of wealth affected your walk with God? Has it been a positive or a negative experience, and why?

What steps can you take to make sure you're seeking lasting wealth in God's kingdom and not just monetary wealth in this life?

Chapter 19

THE TRANSFORMING POWER
OF GOD'S LOVE

Joe often came to work looking scruffy. His clothes had that "slept-in" look. His hair failed to find both a comb and shampoo on many occasions. Sheet marks were marbled across his face. Slurred speech accompanied his disheveled appearance. And all of this usually came with a bonus: a bad attitude.

This was a normal start to Joe's day. During the years he worked for my company, I came to know his struggles well. Joe was raised in a single-parent home. His dad was missing in action. And like so many, Joe sought to soothe his wounds with alcohol, various other substances, and promiscuity.

He loved getting high, but not in the spiritual sense. Honestly, he was one of the roughest and most worldly people I've ever known—and he did little to hide it. He in fact flaunted his "street" look, though he was barely surviving. That said, Joe knew he was trapped in an unhealthy lifestyle, and longed to be healed of all that which ailed both body and spirit.

As a fellow human being, I could sympathize. As a boss, I was frustrated. As a believer, however, I felt compelled to tell him about the good news of the gospel, that there was a better way, and how this superior way included the love and grace offered through Jesus. I went on to explain that Jesus the Christ alone could soothe every hurt, heal every wound, and eventually right every wrong. Thankfully, this was good news to Joe, and he grew more curious over time.

Over a period of a year or so, our conversations leaned in the direction of God's redemptive love, and how that love is laced with real healing power. As a result, I began to see sparkles of belief shining back at me from eyes of hunger. I assumed this life-giving spirit was calling his name, and I was honored to be the conduit for such a message. One day out of the dark grey, Joe said he was ready for real change. Ready to take the step toward God's love, in fact. And I was ready to help him.

Over the next few weeks, we continued in our discussions about the real change that can come about for those who commit their lives to Christ Jesus. We listened to great songs of faith, pondered wonderful truths, and discussed some of what Joe struggled with. I wasn't his counselor, and I didn't pretend to have all the answers. I just kept pointing him to the one who did, and told him about what Jesus had done for me. As the weeks went by, I began to witness a change in Joe that surprised me.

Joe quit drinking and sobered up. He came to work refreshed and well rested. His clothes were cleaner. He cut his hair and washed it more often. His outlook for life brightened as words of bitterness started to wane, and his outward appearance served as evidence. I was both grateful and elated to witness such a transformation in a relatively short period.

Little by little, Joe's real personality surfaced. A sense of humor came forth, one that had been completely smothered by his previous place in life. A delightful spirit arose as if rising from the grave. He was truly a joy to be around, especially considering all that he had left behind. But to my surprise—my shock, really—it didn't last.

With no warning, Joe stopped coming to work. Once we spoke, he made it clear he was going back to his old ways. I struggled to believe that he was willing to walk away from his new life of joy, health, and freedom, seeing things through the life-giving lens of hope. As Joe put it, however: "I missed my old life." He chose to go back to the things that had him addicted and enslaved. I was genuinely stunned, and very disappointed.

False Conversion

There is a hypothesis in Christianity called "false conversion." I don't like the term because if the conversion was false, there was no real conversion in the first place. Therefore, I'm not sure there is such a thing. That said, maybe that's what happened. Only God knows. But with great disappointment, I watched Joe be miraculously delivered from so many harmful things, only to jump right back into the mud pit and soil himself all over again.

Though the whole experience confused me, and in some ways still does, it was a powerful lesson for me. It took me a while to understand what had happened, but in time the truth came into clearer view.

Looking back these many years later, I believe Joe wanted to be a new and improved version of himself, perhaps hoping that would solve his problems and heal the ache that haunted from within. And I understand that way of thinking. Humanly, I suspect we've all wanted that on some level. But God's Word describes the transformation process differently than what we might want for ourselves, or even what we think is reasonable: "He who finds his life will lose it, and he who loses his life for My sake will find it" (Matthew 10:39, NKJV).

Jesus wants to do more than just heal us; He wants to bring us unto a new life that will be lived out for Him. Experiencing the conversion Jesus calls us to requires a willingness to abandon the former self and whatever agenda or purpose we might have had, not merely to have an improved version of it. I believe that's where Joe got off the train. Perhaps when he faced the full reality of what he would have to leave behind, regardless of how much he appreciated his new freedom, he blinked. The idea of giving up self completely is just too much for some. I'm not giving up on Joe, or passing judgment; his destiny is in God's hands. As long as he's alive on this earth, I believe hope remains.

But let me tell you another story—one that I believe better reveals God's idea of real conversion.

Real Transformation

Our paths crossed during the early teen years, and we got along well. But it didn't take long to realize that Larry was a deeply disturbed individual, and one of the angriest people I had ever met. He clashed with his parents, and with just about everyone around him. His level of stubbornness was unsettling, to say the least. With skill and precision, he could make you feel as small as an ant, and quickly make you question the validity of the friendship.

As he grew older, he ended up in multiple inappropriate relationships with women, and flaunted his philandering with pride. He was remarkably dysfunctional, self-centered, and lacking any compassion for others. In His great love and compassion, however, Jesus said, "It is not the healthy who need a doctor, but the sick" (Matthew 9:12).

Some fifty years or so since we've met, I continue to marvel at Larry's transformation. His anger is gone. His compassion for others not only replaced self-centeredness, but morphed into a love and respect for everyone around him. He has a consistent joy about him. His peace lingers, and little rattles him. The spirit that proceeds from him is so starkly different from the guy I once knew that it's getting harder to imagine how he once was.

With Larry, however, there has been no improvement—rather, it has been a replacement of the former self. The "old man" I once knew is simply gone. The only remnants of his passing self are surface personality traits and physical appearance.

I don't see Larry much these days. But when I do, I'm reminded of the power and thoroughness of his transformation, God's way—one that has touched every part of his being and addressed every flaw to one degree or another. He's not perfect, or a finished work. Whenever I see him, however, I'm reminded of the miraculous change that occurs when our loving God gets a hold of someone. That's how I know his transformation is real. He hasn't gotten "better"; rather, a new spirit altogether rules his heart.

Jesus says we'll know people by their fruit—not by what they say or what they claim, but by the lives they live out over time. Larry's "fruit" is astoundingly evident all these decades later. His old self was not merely improved but replaced with a new spirit, a new person. This kind of fruit and transformation can only be brought about through our loving Savior Jesus.

A Transformation God Desires

One of the reasons God wants an entirely new person is because we're being designed for an entirely new kingdom: the soon-coming kingdom of God. But there's another crucial reason, and that is that the human mind, even at its very best, is at enmity against

God. Apart from God, the human mind is incapable of nothing but hostility toward Him. Therefore, a new person entirely has to be created.

> Therefore, if anyone is in Christ, he is a new creation; old things have passed away; behold, all things have become new. (2 Corinthians 5:17, NKJV)

The conversion process takes time. To change from a resistant human spirit to an agreeable eternal spirit is a lifetime process for most. But when it's complete, it will have no trace of the former human self. All pride, pleasures of the flesh, and arrogance will slowly erode from those in the transformation process. It's a beautiful thing to witness in others, and to experience personally.

However, I also want you to see that this transformation process crescendos when we come to rest in God's love. Anything short of the knowledge of godly love simply won't do.

> We know that "We all possess knowledge." But knowledge puffs up while love builds up. Those who think they know something do not yet know as they ought to know. But whoever loves God is known by God. (1 Corinthians 8:1–3)

A Light on a Hill

Jesus made an interesting statement about what He desires to do with those who have been transformed into His likeness:

> You are the light of the world. A city that is set on a hill cannot be hidden. Nor do they light a lamp and put it under a basket, but on a lampstand, and it gives light to

all who are in the house. Let your light so shine before men, that they may see your good works and glorify your Father in heaven. (Matthew 5:14–16, NKJV)

God will transform faithful believers into something remarkable—and that will be part of our witness. Some think our witness is in religious behavior, being right about everything, or having a high degree of biblical knowledge. Others think it's primarily about just having faith and being as good as possible. But the Word of God narrows it down: "And now these three remain: faith, hope and love. But the greatest of these is love" (1 Corinthians 13:13).

We've addressed this fact in various ways throughout this book. As we come closer to the end of *The Way He Loves*, however, we must bring this point home. Being a loving Christian is not just the most important part of representing our Savior Jesus—it's also our final test.

The Final Test in Love

In order to love our neighbor as ourselves, we must have a healthy sense of humility; "self" must be denied. Why? Because people will not always show us love back, even when we're being loving. I've learned firsthand that the world may like and appreciate a loving spirit, but not everyone will respect it. Some, in fact, will try to take advantage of it and have no intention of returning that love. Because of this, our own pride has to be set aside in order to indiscriminately bring love to others.

We can't walk around being overly sensitive and taking everything personally. And we certainly can't have the attitude that we'll withhold love and courtesy because someone may not return that love or kindness. When others are disrespectful, we still must treat them with a spirit of love and courtesy. If we're driven by ego or pride, that won't happen. The Lord has certainly had to work on me in this regard. The truth is, there will always be room for growth in this area.

The spirit of the world sees love as weak, needy, and nothing more than appeasement. We know, of course, that the truth is the opposite. Godly love is the most bold and powerful force in the universe, as we have shown in previous chapters, and has everything to do with the strength of God. But for now it's delivered in the form of a whisper, and sometimes in seemingly weak and unimpressive people. However, like a blade of grass growing up through a crack in a concrete sidewalk, love will prevail. No other force in the universe can stop the love of God.

It's easier to seek respect and accolades for having a formal education of some kind, to hold various titles, and to have great achievements for others to see and admire—even having a big ministry in which one can boast. There's nothing wrong with any of these, but if you need these to feel confident or useful to God, you may be looking for approval from the wrong source.

The final test of being a loving person, therefore, is to be willing to set all that aside—because, to be known simply as someone who treats everyone with love and kindness is not admired in our world. Love, however, is not an option for the Christian who wants to walk in God's will. If you achieve every other attribute of God but fail to be a loving person, you are simply not rising to God's potential for you, or the level He requires. How important is being a loving person to God?

> And this is love: that we walk in obedience to his commands. As you have heard from the beginning, his command is that you walk in love. (2 John 6)

Wow. It's astonishing that we can be religious and do a lot of good works, and still manage to not love others. But we shouldn't be too surprised in this regard. God's Word makes clear that we can do all these noble things and yet refuse to humble ourselves before God, surrendering the self. If we don't get around to genuinely loving God and others, no other trait we've picked up along the way can make up for it. But when we are willing to surrender the self along with its ego, we become more useful to God. And when we do, life gets really good.

Learning to Trust in God's Love

When I consider my own journey with Jesus, and how difficult my own childhood was, I often think about how slow I was in coming around to really trusting in God's love for me personally. As I do so increasingly over time, however, I can see the direct impact it has on how well I love both God and others. The more we trust in God's love for us personally, the more equipped we are to know what real love is, and then be able to take it to others. This allows us to love others in truth, not just emotionally or romantically. Therefore, learning to trust in God's faithful love and letting that love bear its fruit in us over time is paramount to the reality of the Christian walk, along with our witness to that reality.

But if we are not experiencing God's love, if we're not letting His Spirit rule our hearts, we will not have that love for others. And then we may be nothing more than religious zealots.

The Highest Level of Living

There's great reward in placing all our hope and well-being in the hands of our loving God. It is simply the pinnacle of the Christian experience. It's rewarding to have faith in all things, to study and learn Christian doctrine, to well up in hope for this or that. But nothing compares to having a heart filled with love from our God, and then to have that love and compassion toward a fellow human being.

This is true because godly love is not just our calling—it's our fuel. Yes, we live by God's Spirit, but the essence of that Spirit is love. Never am I more alive than when I love with a godly love.

Seeking to Understand the Way He Loves

As we learn to trust God's love for us and to bring that love to others, only then are we in the position to understand God's love and to see it for what it is. After all, God's Word tells us, "God is love." And we're called to emulate Him. I've learned to pray, however, "God, teach me to love the way you love." He's in the process of answering that prayer, and there's certainly room for improvement. Little by little, however, I'm being transformed into the heart of God, and knowing what it means to walk with God. I hope you'll receive the call and do the same.

> His pleasure is not in the strength of the horse, nor his delight in the legs of the warrior; the Lord delights in those who fear him, who put their hope in his unfailing love. (Psalm 147:10–11)

Reflection Questions

How do you feel about God not just wanting to improve the human-you, but to create a whole new person in you—one designed for an entirely different kind of kingdom?

Are there parts of yourself you have not yielded to God, or any areas that you are not letting God in that He may heal you? If so, how can you start letting God into those areas?

In what ways can you see God transforming you into His own image?

Chapter 20

PREPARING HEARTS TO BECOME AGENTS OF GOD'S LOVE

The 1990s were coming to a climactic end. Y2K was on everybody's mind. And the idea the world might suddenly end dominated the airways, and the fears of many. Though I had my concerns about a decade, a century, and a millennium coming to a simultaneous end, I did my best to keep the hype from getting in my own spirit.

I was single at the time. The university I had been attending had closed its doors a couple of years earlier, and nearly everyone I knew had left the area. While trying to map out my next move in life, I didn't want to just hover. So, I decided to do some good in the community I would temporarily call home, ending up with a short stint at a local soup kitchen. While there, I learned the lesson of a lifetime concerning the relationship between good deeds and the condition of one's heart.

More Than Just Soup

The kitchen itself was well designed and commercial grade. Every pot and pan you could think of filled the storage shelves and stainless-steel countertops. And the cafeteria style setup made for an efficient operation.

I served in the meal line. And as the poor and struggling came through, I offered up cheerful hellos and a welcoming smile. After bellies were filled, and a few frowns turned upward, everyone was encouraged to walk down the hall to hear a sermon in the chapel. But to my surprise, I soon realized there was a spirit that filled the place that lurked in contrast to the work we were there to do.

Within a day or two of my being there, it became apparent there was infighting among the volunteers and some of the staff. As I quietly kept to my assigned tasks, I overheard some of the staff and crew talking badly about each other behind their backs. Foul language was tossed about like typical fare in an R-rated movie. The strife was thicker than the pudding we offered for dessert. And a competitive spirit dominated, and not in a good way. With no attempt to conceal the contempt they held for each other, the chaos was in full view for everyone to see—including those we were there to serve.

Some of those precious souls who had come in for respite from a harsh world were forced to witness another form of brutality: division among brethren. Clearly uncomfortable with what they were hearing, they did their best to ignore it. Facial expressions of surprise and rolling eyes, however, revealed their lack of approval. And to no one's surprise, many were reluctant to go into the chapel after their meal.

After witnessing such a heavy dose of the world in what was supposed to be an example of the contrary, I could not stay there very long. I feared their poison might get into my own spirit. Besides, there was pressure for me to take sides and join in the harpooning of fellow believers. I abstained. Pleaded the fifth. And fled the scene, never looking back.

Those who came to that soup kitchen received some good food, but were not fed the unifying and loving Spirit of God. And though I couldn't see through the weeds of confusion and disappointment at the time, a question eventually arose from that unfortunate event: What matters most: the good deed one performs, or the state of one's heart while performing that deed?

Before we look closer at taking God's love to a hurting world, it's crucial that we answer this question.

Our Troubled World

When I look around at this world of ours and ponder all its troubles and ills, I ask myself: What can I *do* to make a difference? I'm sure you do the same thing. And I can think of much good that comes from that simple question. That said, I've learned a profound truth when it comes to doing good in the world around us, and it is this: lasting and right influence does not begin with action. Rather, it begins with who we *are* as people, and the spirit and attitude that wells up from within us.

Our actions, for the most part, are expressions of our inner person, a reflection of who and what we already are. Therefore, what we end up doing and how we treat others in general is a direct manifestation of the content of our hearts.

Contrary to what many believe, our nature is not created by action. Doing good deeds does not make our hearts better. No, only God can change our hearts via the Holy Spirit of God. Carrying out right actions can influence or stir up what's already in us, but in themselves cannot transform the heart. If they could, we wouldn't need the redeeming work of God in us in order to change.

Therefore, perhaps the question is not "What are you doing with your life?" Rather: "What is the condition of your inner person?" Whatever the answer to that question is will determine what you'll end up *doing* with and for others over time. Are we being ruled by an altruistic and helpful spirit of godly love? If we are, we'll naturally live out a life of service, encouragement, and compassion for others. And our good deeds will naturally align with that loving spirit.

A person who focuses on right action primarily, and whose heart is not necessarily aligned with that action, can fake it for only so long. I've simply lived as a Christian too long to be fooled by any other idea about the health of one's heart. I've faked it on occasion, and I've watched others fake it, and in the long run it does not produce good fruit. Only our commitment to our God, along with the redemption process, will allow Him to perform our needed heart surgery, creating authentic change. When a loving spirit precedes good actions, we're set to make a lasting difference for the kingdom of God. This is important because for now, we are God's only personal representation of His coming kingdom.

> Once, on being asked by the Pharisees when the kingdom of God would come, Jesus replied, "The coming of the kingdom of God is not something that can be observed, nor will people say, 'Here it is,' or 'There it is,' because the kingdom of God is in your midst." (Luke 17:20–21)

In this scripture, Jesus seems to be taking the emphasis concerning His kingdom away from an action or event, and placing it on the person of Jesus Himself and those who were His, those who housed His Spirit. When you look at what the Gospels reveal, people were moved and witnessed to simply by being in Jesus's presence. Yes, he performed good works, but people of the day knew there was a different spirit ruling His heart. That alone was a major part of His witness.

> When Jesus had finished saying these things, the crowds were amazed at his teaching, because he taught as one who had authority, and not as their teachers of the law. (Matthew 7:28–29)

Followers of Jesus today have that same Spirit moving through them. As God's kingdom is first revealed in the hearts of His followers who live by this loving Spirit, an accurate expression of His kingdom will be revealed through us. Our witness to the heart and love of God isn't necessarily about building a large ministry, carrying out heroic acts of goodwill, or doing physical works, as important as these are. And it's not always going to be something we can point to "over here" or "over there." Therefore, we can't live in a paradigm that suggests that our actions are the only thing that matters. Good works have their place in our love for others, of course, but we're called to a higher plane. And it begins with being loving and Spirit-filled believers in Christ Jesus. Only from this place will we bring a spirit of love and hope that contradicts the spirit of this world—including the religious spirit of works and ritual.

People need to see a consistency between who we are internally and the good things we're doing outwardly. One ends up confirming the other, and becomes a very powerful and effective witness.

Being Single-Hearted

Another crucial aspect of representing the light and heart of God is making sure we do not have a duplicitous heart. Duplicity is when a person lives in such a way that their inner thoughts, what they say outwardly, and their actions are all misaligned. In other words, they are not consistent in what they claim to believe, and the life they live out. They may speak of the importance of a moral life, for instance, while secretly living out an immoral and compromising life. The world is filled with people who live this way.

But when we are committed to being people of a single heart and mind, and live in a way that is consistent with our stated beliefs, a powerful spirit emits from us. This is a crucial part of our witness. If we're not living single-heartedly, we're considered hypocrites, which dishonors our God and invalidates our witness.

This doesn't mean we have to be perfect and wait until every issue we're dealing with is solved; otherwise none of us would qualify to serve. However, we get an idea of how important it is to God that we live out the life we claim to believe through Jesus's words: "Hypocrite! First remove the plank from your own eye, and then you will see clearly to remove the speck from your brother's eye" (Matthew 7:5, NKJV).

Can you imagine the harm done if we do good works in Jesus's name but come across as complete phonies to the people we're serving? As hypocrites? The thought of such a blunder should disgust and horrify us all, because it involves deception and deceit.

And don't think God isn't aware of our nature, and whether we're being true to Him, ourselves, and others.

> When Jesus saw Nathanael approaching, he said of him, "Here truly is an Israelite in whom there is no deceit."

"How do you know me?" Nathanael asked.

Jesus answered, "I saw you while you were still under the fig tree before Philip called you." (John 1:47–48)

We're called to be the real thing, single-hearted and without a deceitful nature—to make sure our hearts, actions, and personal lives align with one another. The more I've worked on this personally, the better my life goes, and the better my witness.

If the loving spirit of mercy and kindness is not flowing through your being, ask God to help you deal with this. If there's something in your life that you know is inconsistent with your faith in Jesus, be prepared to make changes as our loving God brings them to light. God is always faithful to forgive, equip, and empower us for real change.

It's crucial to do this because if the love of God is not freely flowing through us, if there is any barrier to that love, then judgment and criticism is more likely to flow. And people can sense which place we're coming from, however subtly. God will not work through someone who lives as a hypocrite or is relying on mere human nature.

Before I go to serve, meet with friends, help those in need, counsel someone, or whatever, I've learned to check my heart before God and ask Him to make sure I'm going in with the right perspective of heart, mind, and spirit. And He faithfully answers that prayer.

Treating Everyone with Dignity

I have worked in various other soup kitchens and shelters in the years before and after that unfortunate experience above, and they were all wonderful experiences—not only with the amazing people I got to serve with, but in getting to know some of those we were there to encourage. In these experiences over the years, I've learned that there is something far more important to most of them than food and being preached at, and that is being shown kindness, dignity, and acceptance. This is God's heart, and the way He loves.

I have seen the poor and homeless refuse help from some because they didn't feel respected or valued. If someone feels looked down upon or merely handled, they may not only distrust some who may be trying to help, but just might have contempt for our Savior Jesus. But when someone comes to them with the Spirit and heart of God, their faces and souls light up as they recognize what they crave the most.

This is true of course with people in all walks of life, not just the poor or struggling but even healthy and successful people. Therefore, our witness is to everyone we encounter, wherever we encounter them. In addition, we don't insult them by trying to fix them, which is often construed as unacceptance. When we understand that we can't fix people, that it's not necessarily our job to solve their problems but to merely show that we love and value them, real transformation can happen. Yes, various ways in which to help practically may come to light, and we can act on them should they present themselves. But laying that foundation of acceptance from the beginning is the best evidence of God's loving nature. We are to be agents of God's love.

Yes, there are some who are there to milk the system and couldn't care less for the love and goodness of God, or kindness from others. Therefore, it's good to remember that we only plant the seed and water it, and that only God can cause it to grow. Our part is making sure our hearts are in the right place and to serve others in love, acceptance, and from a place of integrity. Whether

God uses that, or how He uses that, is His prerogative, and will be according to His will.

We Are the Ministry of God

I've long let go of the idea that I must create a large and visible ministry in order to be a conduit for God's love, or, that there must be some visible evidence of an organized religious entity outside myself. The truth is, we *are* the ministry. True believers and those who possess God's Spirit are the very house of God, and the message that God desires to project in this world through followers of Christ Jesus.

As I grow in this perspective, it's easier to understand that the work of God is in us and expressed through us personally. As we do, the light of God's love and hope for the world will be expressed in our very person, and in all we do.

Our Work Begins with Neighbor One

This may sound obvious to some, but "neighbor one" is our family, and those closest to us. Bringing God's amazing love to the world around us begins here. I've known and witnessed too many Christian families who have been neglected in the name of a "ministry" or "God's work" the father was involved in. It's practically become a cliché. So many pastor's kids have been lonely, neglected, and out of sorts with others around them. And the ones I knew personally were nearly always disconnected from a healthy relationship with their fathers. That should never be the case.

In fact, if we let God's Word convey God's very heart on this issue, the children of pastors, ministers, and those who lead various ministries should be the most nurtured, happy, confident, and loved children around. No matter our calling, there is simply never an excuse for not loving and providing for those whom God has put in our trust. And this is never truer than with our own spouses and children.

> But if anyone does not provide for his own, and especially for those of his household, he has denied the faith and is worse than an unbeliever. (1 Timothy 5:8, NKJV)

I'm not Catholic, but I like the way Mother Teresa put it: "If you want to change the world, go home and love your family."

As we consider the condition of our own hearts before God, the next chapter takes a closer look at taking God's love to others in a way that makes a real impact.

Reflection Questions

How does a right heart before God supersede good works?

How would you describe the condition of your own heart, especially in relation to reaching out and helping others?

As you help others, where do you feel a healthy connection of love and compassion for those hurting, along with a desire to want to improve their life or situation?

What areas could you improve or need to grow in, in regard to taking the love of God to others with the right motives?

Chapter 21

TAKING GOD'S LOVE TO A LOVE-STARVED WORLD

*H*e was meaner than a cat with its tail caught in the door. He yelled at his grown kids when they came to visit, and he could empty a bucket of sunshine quicker than anyone I knew. But we assumed he was in our orbit for a reason. Therefore, we felt compelled to show the love and goodness of God to this less than jovial man, and hopefully be a witness in the process.

As we reached out, we didn't talk to him about Jesus. We didn't point out his sins or how he might do things better. We just looked for ways to be good to him, and hopefully improve his life. And searching for an area of need didn't take long.

The trees, bushes, and other vegetation around his house had been neglected for years. The overgrowth was so thick that major sections of his house hadn't been seen for years. So one day I asked if we could clean things up for him, and he agreed. We organized a group of friends one Saturday soon after and began to trim trees, cut back bushes, and remove tons of undergrowth. And the difference it made was tremendous. But the effect this had on the man was the real reward.

One day after much work had been done, he walked outside, looked around, and saw the difference it had made. And with a facial expression of rare gratitude he simply stated, "Thank you for being such thoughtful Christian people." Like I said, we never said anything about Jesus or Christianity; we just kindly tried to help along with a joyful spirit, and God did the rest.

On another occasion, there was a young man my wife and I were doing some home repairs for. He suffered from chronic back problems along with other ailments. And one day while working in his house, I asked if he would like me and my wife to pray for him, for his back issues specifically. He sternly refused, saying that it was not necessary. That night, however, my wife and I prayed for him in private just before going to bed, and didn't think any more about it.

The next day while back in his house finishing up our work, he came up to me excited and standing upright, in a better mood than usual. With rare enthusiasm, he asked, "Did you happen to pray for me last night?" A little surprised at the question, I hesitated and said, "Yes, actually we did." He then said passionately, "I knew it. Your prayers healed my back." He went on to tell me that he woke up that morning with no pain or stiffness in his back for the first time in years. And he gave the full credit to our God.

The truth is that he had faith, he was exercising that faith, and that's what healed him. That's how powerful helping people can be. It may be as simple as helping in a way that stirs up what's already in their hearts.

My point is not to bring attention to what my wife and I have done, rather to what our God can do when we are willing to be agents of His love. As you look for simple ways to help others, especially with a caring spirit, God may very well use that to bless someone in a very personal way. There's a reason why this may be one of the best approaches I've ever tried.

The Principle of Discovery

When being an effective witness for God, I have found that few words are needed. In fact, the less the better; my witness is more effective when I don't preach at all. Rather, I give room for that person to see the spirit of Jesus on their own, and then let them point Him out. I like to think of this as the principle of discovery.

When we allow others to experience something good such as our love and treatment of them, and then let them discover on their own that it's the Spirit of God, they are more receptive. If you put the name of Jesus out there before they get a chance to see your heart and the good you might be doing, they just might be robbed of the wonderful experience of discovering Jesus on their own. When we deny someone room for their own discovery, they are often more defensive. They may then become more likely to reject the name of Jesus, *and* our good deeds.

There's more to this point, however. I believe it's God's preferred way to work through His people. Instead of trying to control the outcome, or tell others what they should believe, we instead allow God's Spirit to guide things as He wishes. We know so little of people and their lives, who they are, and what they need. But God knows everything and exactly what one needs. We're wise to trust this to God. In my interaction with others, I have found this approach to be far better, and the experience to be more authentic.

As we resist the temptation to preach to people, or to throw the name of Jesus in their faces, our treatment of them will speak for itself. You can trust this. After all, when people tell us what we *should* believe, aren't we all a little skeptical? Isn't it true that most of us don't like being told upfront what to think, what we should believe, or what we should do? Don't we all like to have the room to discover things on our own and make up our own minds? Of course we do. This nugget of wisdom is worth pondering for a while, primarily because it speaks to loving others and treating them in the way we'd want to be loved and treated.

There's a time for words, but there's a reason that the Word of God puts the emphasis on deeds with a right heart rather than just preaching. I once had an employee who had fallen on hard times, so a colleague of mine delivered a bag of groceries to his house. The employee was in the front yard with his kids when my friend arrived. He just got out of the truck and handed him some groceries and only said, "I heard you were having a hard time right now, so I brought you some groceries." My friend was shocked at what happened next. This tough, prideful, and hardened blue-collar worker broke down crying right in front of my friend. After shedding tears of gratefulness, he said in broken speech, "You're one of those Christians, aren't you?" The witness just happened, and God got the glory. The Holy Spirit was at work in that man, and my friend was honored to be a part of it.

When a person shows up with a right heart and God's Spirit, people somehow know it. If the Spirit of God is truly in you, God will use your witness. If we keep looking for ways to help others and treat them well, God will do the rest.

A drifter once came up to me at a convenience store and asked for money. But unlike so many asking for help, he was willing to work for it. I could instantly see that he was mentally challenged, and about thirty-five years old. My heart went out to him because he had that look of being a small fish in a sea of barracudas. So instead of giving him a job, I took him to a local restaurant for lunch.

As we sat down with our food, I wanted to hear his story. I asked about his past and why he was so far away from home. He struggled to put together a coherent timeline of events, which is common among the homeless. The best I could gather was that he was physically and emotionally abused by his own family, and probably had been all his life. His mental limitations appeared to make him a target, even from his own family members. He was thousands of miles away from home in hopes of surviving. Very hard to hear.

As we enjoyed our meal together, few words were exchanged. I began to wonder if we were going to have any real dialogue, or whether I would have any positive influence in his life. After doing my best to generate a conversation, his eyes grew a little watery right before he said, in a childlike way, "No one has ever sat down with me to just have a meal together."

This happened about twenty years ago as I write this, but still hits me pretty hard. There's a lot of pain out there, a lot of hurting folks. And as my wife has confirmed after working in the hospital system for almost a decade, most abuse cases are from family members. Truly tragic.

This all reminds me that a simple kindness can go a long way, even toward strangers. We never know what people are going through. I was unable to do anything that would constitute real change in his life that day, but I know God can. And who knows, maybe it was a turning point. God can use the smallest of occurrences to speak to any of us, and certainly to those who seem to be in helpless situations.

I have a friend who reaches out to people within his own neighborhood, looking for ways to be a help wherever there's a need; it could be just about anything. He's amazing. Who does that? I'm so inspired by my friend who just goes door to door, asking if he can be of service. And he's done this for years. What a light he is. But he does it from a humble and kind spirit. People love that about him. His caring and humble heart is as much the witness as his deeds. He is truly a light on a hill.

The condition of one's heart, however, works in both directions. Another friend we'll call Bill once was invited to hear a prominent Christian author, one of the most well-known preachers of our time, speak at a luncheon. After the event was over, and after hearing about all the great accomplishments this preacher was known for, Bill decided to approach the pastor in hopes of meeting him, shaking his hand, and thanking him for a great speech and all that he had accomplished. Bill was very inspired by this man.

On the way over, however, the preacher saw my friend Bill coming toward him and suddenly started staring at him. At first Bill thought he was just watching him approach, knowing they were about to meet. However, Bill soon began to feel uncomfortable. The famous preacher began to look Bill up and down with a look of disgust and disapproval; his body language was that of disdain. As a result, a spirit of judgment and criticism raced through Bill's soul. He stopped and decided not to approach the minister. Bill said he had never felt so despised before, and didn't understand why.

From that day on, the great deeds and accomplishments of this pastor meant very little to Bill. When he recounts the story, this minister's great works don't even come to mind. As he told the story, all Bill could think about was that this great man of God despised him and seemed to loathe his very presence. Yet amazingly, Bill never criticized the preacher or said anything negative about him. He mostly just shared the surprise and pain.

Great accomplishments in God's work are good, but if they're not laced with a heart of mercy, acceptance, and love, they lose their meaning—and can create confusion and pain within a message of profound contradiction. If a spirit of genuine love does not dominate our outlook on others, a spirit of criticism will fill that void. In reality, it's one or the other. In the years since, Bill has been unable to fully embrace the Christian message.

All the World Is Our Mission Field

No matter our station in life, the whole world is fertile ground for being ambassadors for God's amazing love. The workplace, the places where we shop, go out to eat, have the oil changed in our car, etc.—people everywhere are starving for interaction with others who are filled with the light of God, regardless of whether they can articulate that or not.

Being loving can be as simple as engaging others as we go about our day. The level of disconnectedness in our culture is profoundly sad, and deeply rooted in our society. I have the best conversations with complete strangers, and it usually only lasts a few minutes. But someone has to take the initiative, and most are waiting for the other person to act. With God's help and spirit, we can go against the grain and reach out to people in all kinds of situations. It's incredibly rewarding to do so.

In my own walk, I'm learning the joy of making the move and initiating connectivity, which is not a natural part of my personality. As with many of us writers, we can easily hunker down in our writing. I've had to work at it. But as I do, the spirits of both myself and others are lifted. There's a lot wrong with our world, but there's also a lot right with it. And our good nature toward others serves as evidence to the good still in this world. We all need more of this kind of interaction. You can be a part of it. And I believe our God prefers to show that life and love directly through His people.

Don't walk around as a sourpuss with your head hanging down. Smile. Look up, and look for opportunities to engage people. This is part of sharing the love and excellence of God—even if it only lasts a brief time.

We have to be wise and careful, however. There are some folks that we should avoid. Not everyone is safe to interact with, which is why I almost always interact with people when there are other folks nearby, and with people who seem generally healthy. Approaching people on the street or in an isolated environment is not wise, and not worth the risk. We leave that to professional social workers and those who do this in groups. I suggest interacting with others in safe environments where people gather in general: grocery stores, a coffee shop, the doctor's office, with people we work with, do business with, go to school with, or hire to do work for us. That said, if you ever feel uncomfortable or that weary gut feeling is sending up alarms, listen to it and don't approach that person. This has become a sad reality in our world.

Great interactions with people can happen anywhere, especially according to the guidelines stated above. And as we engage and interact with others with healthy caution and wisdom, we can become useful agents of God's love.

Be Generous with God's Generosity

As I look for safe opportunities to be good to others, I like to think of it as being generous with what God has given me. One thought that helped me come out of my own shell was that I had no right to hold back from others what God had so generously given me. If God has been good to us but we withhold that goodness from others, we're being stingy. Our lives will not rise to their potential, as a result. Be generous with what God has been generous to you with, and you'll thrive.

Increasingly I'm anxious to share with others the amazing hope, joy, and goodness that God has filled me with. He's been so good to me, has forgiven so much, and there's simply no story I'd rather tell. Writing is one of those outlets for me. What are some outlets for telling others how God has been good to you? Whatever your outlet or platform is, you'll brighten people's day, inspire them to rise higher, and believe that God is good and can forgive and bless them too.

I'm surprised really at how some Christians receive so much from God but stay only to themselves. Why? If that is you, now is the time for change. Go out there and share God's amazing love with others. We don't have to do this in an awkward, weird, or pushy way—rather, in a way that comes across naturally when the opportunity is right, and with those we naturally come in contact with. We all have a circle of influence. Use that influence to be good to people in such a way that shows the love and goodness of God. Really, is there a higher calling?

When the Kingdom of God Is Near

People can sense much more than we may sometimes realize. If you're walking around with the loving Spirit of God and you're open to engaging others when natural and appropriate, people sense that the kingdom of God is near, even if they can't quite put their finger on it. Do not underestimate what can happen when we reach out to others like this. For those available and willing, God can do a work anytime and with anyone; just be available for that moment. Just about anyone can be moved by people who have a spirit in them that is truly alive.

Years ago I had a business meeting with a guy we were thinking of hiring. As we sat in the board room and our discussions had come to an end, I sensed there was something more on his mind and that he needed to share something with me on a personal level. The truth was, I needed to end the meeting and get on with my day; I was running behind and had a lot to do. But in my spirit, I felt compelled to just sit back, shut my mouth, and let the conversation take its own course. I set my things down and embraced an attitude of "just wait and see what happens."

In a matter of seconds, and out of nowhere, he began to tell me about an item he saw for sale in an antique shop that reminded him of his now deceased wife. The item was very expensive, but he knew that if his wife were still with him, she would want him to buy it for her. So he did. She had died about three years earlier, and he was having a hard time learning to live without her. This item brought back some good memories and made him feel connected again, but it also brought some pain and he needed to tell someone.

Then, the story took a different direction. He used the story he just told me as a springboard to share how God had really been taking care of him through the years since her passing, and that God drew him closer in the process. He was learning to rely on God more and more for every need.

I sat there, nearly speechless. I was not prepared for how this man's story would move me; there was a lump in my throat. But the highest honor was having been chosen to hear that which was on this man's heart. Had I rushed off or failed to listen to that inner voice, I would have missed it.

Though I'm glad I was there for him, he had no idea how he was there for me. Even though I was already a believer, his story witnessed to me in a powerful way. I left that meeting with my own faith bolstered, and absolutely overjoyed at how God shows such comforting love toward hurting people, and in such personal ways.

The Love Deficit

One way we can sum up the world we live in is that it has a major love deficit. Therefore, when we engage others, so they feel important, valued, and appreciated as friends, even in the hustle and bustle of our day, a connection happens. A void just may be filled. Slowing down a little, taking extra time for someone, giving them the time and space to open up and share what's going on inside, is a tremendous gift—although, I fear, an increasingly rare one.

When ordinary people interact in an ordinary way, on an ordinary day, an extraordinary event can occur as someone comes in contact with God's very kingdom. Remember, the kingdom is in our midst, in us. This is truly one of the deepest joys in life, and it's entirely about our willingness to be a conduit for God's love in a rather loveless world—and sometimes in the spur of the moment.

I don't try and corral people to live or act the way I think they should. God holds the heart of every human being in His hands, and it's His business what He does with them. If a conversation goes further and the door opens to encourage a different approach to life I'm ready for it, and I've done that. But I've also learned to not force it. This approach is important to our God because He desires to inspire people to seek Him willingly, not coerce them.

As people of faith, we know that only God can call people to repentance, change their lives, and compel them to live as Christ Jesus wants them to live. Therefore, the distinction between being a loving person and a controlling person is worth noting.

If God wants someone to make a change in their lives, turn from some lifestyle choice, to walk away from a bad habit, or even join a particular group of Christians, He knows how to get them there. And if he wants you or me to be involved in that, let's make sure it happens organically and with a right and trusting spirit.

Some are called to lead large ministries and form great institutions of faith, but most of us are called to mind the trenches and walk the fields of this world. In doing so, we're simply called to reflect the heart of God in all we do, and before all with whom we come in contact.

A God of Love

Those of us in the Christian faith know we were once lost in our sins, and in need of a Savior. But this is just the beginning, and far from the whole picture.

Our God is a God of love, and has profound love for each of us personally. Since my walk began in 1981, I have known nothing but the kindness, patience, encouragement, hope, and faithful friendship from our God of love. As He's called me to repent of my sins and clean up my life, His faithful love and acceptance has always been in the mix. As a result, there's nothing that gives me more joy and purpose today than our loving God—and that includes bringing this wonderful truth in love to others. I hope you'll join me in this pursuit.

Our Best Gift to the World

I'm not sure whether the world has gotten nastier during my lifetime or if the megaphones that spew the darkness in the world have simply gotten louder; I suspect the latter. What I am sure of, however, is that our world is hurting on many fronts, and it needs the one and only antidote for the poison that is now systemic. That healing potion is the love and faithfulness of our amazing God.

I don't believe the answer is just more preaching, the building of more churches necessarily, or believers becoming more religious. I do believe that the answer lies in the real love our God has for a love-starved world. We can be agents of that love, and live in such a way that serves as evidence to that love.

Keep being your best. Be a person of excellence. Let the goodness, perfection, and joy of God fill your being and overflow to those around you—and reject anything to the contrary. But most of all, be a loving believer.

As you consider what your life will be about moving forward, what you'll become, and what your purpose in life will be, I want you to leave you with two questions:

> What could possibly be more important than God's healing love for our hurting world?
>
> What possible calling could be higher than being an agent for God's healing love?
>
> *Praise be to the Lord, for he showed me the wonders of his love.* (Psalm 31:21)

Reflection Questions

Do you think it's fair to say that the only right motive with others is the motive to love in truth? Why or why not?

In what ways have you been bringing God's love, kindness, and acceptance to others?

Where is there room for growth, or new ways you can bring this love to others in your circle of influence?

Are you prepared to bring God's love to others at a moment's notice, or whenever that need presents itself? Explain.

Contact the Author

If you want to share your experiences with the author, you can email me, Preston Rentz, at preston@prestonrentz.com. I'd love to hear your reactions—and your responses to how God has been calling you forward as you've been reading.

ENDNOTES

Chapter 1: The Desert's Heart

[1] Stephen Orr, "An Incredible Story of Survival in Fierce County," InDaily, July 6, 2018, https://indaily.com.au//inreview/books-and-poetry/2018/07/06/incredible-story-survival-fierce-country; Sue Short, "How Did Bogucki Survive?", ABC-PM, August 23, 1999, https://www.abc.net.au/pm/stories/s45783.htm.

[2] Short, "How Did Bogucki Survive?"

Chapter 2: Beyond the Clay

[3] *Steve McQueen: American Icon*, directed by Jon Erwin and Ben Small-bone (New York: Virgil Films, 2018), DVD.

[4] Greg Laurie, *Steve McQueen: The Salvation of an American Icon* (Grand Rapids, MI: Zondervan, 2017).

[5] *Steve McQueen: American Icon.*

Chapter 9: A Backdrop for Love

[6] Michael Martinez, "Widow of American Teacher Forgives Attackers Who Killed Her Husband in Libya," CNN, December 20, 2013, https://www.cnn.com/2013/12/20/us/libya-widow-teacher-forgives-attackers.

Printed in the United States
by Baker & Taylor Publisher Services